MEASURING SUCCESS

MEASURING SUCCESS

A PRACTICAL GUIDE TO KPIS

GREG BRISENDINE

For Chad

FOREWORD

I don't think it's a coincidence that the best measurement consultants I've known in my two decades in this industry were artists. Early in my career I was mentored by some remarkably talented statisticians – mathematics PhDs with masterful understandings of the nuance of analytics and the ability to spot statistical pitfalls and process errors with laser-like precision. They would seemingly disappear into their cubicles for days at a time, mining through mountains of data to locate problems that the organization didn't even know it had. And despite bringing forth defensible and informed recommendations – wrung free of as much uncertainty as mathematically possible – their proposals almost always fell on deaf ears. Meanwhile, the people who always seemed to make the most impact were the consultants who were also artists. Because (as you are about to learn from this book) what we measure is reflective of what we value.

Statisticians derive value from metrics.

Artists derive *metrics* from *what we most value*. (And *then* they do the statistics part.)

Who better than an artist to consult with people on a human level? To identify their most important values? To disassemble a convoluted work state, to isolate and explicate the tangled web of motives and self-protections and strategies and kindnesses, and to distill that into a recognizable, definable set of performance indicators? It is a patently "human" process – one that my early mentors regularly bypassed in the search for problems hidden within the data. But the consultants-who-were-also-artists were perfectly suited for this work, as they already sought these answers in everything they do.

Greg Brisendine is one of those people. He's a consultant, and analyst, a strategist, and a statistician. But he's also a poet, a playwright, a storyteller, and a performer. This book is his testimony to the importance of identifying our values. And measuring them. And optimizing them. This book teaches that if we are honest with ourselves, we can identify a few key performance indicators that will maximize our efforts to achieve our goals. This is not a typical "business measurement" book, focused on how to measure behaviors only inasmuch as they contribute to some ill-defined ROI that you, the reader, are expected to believe will save your job and make you the hero of your organization. This book is not for people who want to prove their numeric value through ROI; this book is for people who want to make things better.

Fortunately for all readers, Greg is one of the great guides through this process. Like all great guides, his goal is to ensure that you feel empowered from the first step. If you are confused or intimidated by statistics or analytics or strategy, or if you are not in touch with what you value, Greg addresses the entire process with the experience of a master, and the gentle-but-firm touch of the poet that he is. The process of improvement should be inspiring, after all, and Greg will help ease your fears and inspire you to change things for the better – in your team, in your organization, in your life.

Measurement is not easy, but it shouldn't be inaccessible. *Measuring Success* is evidence that it doesn't have to be.

This is Greg, at his best. Speaking like an artist: engaging, inspiring, and easy to understand.

Helping us take inventory of our values, our behaviors, and their measurable results.

Helping us define our successes.

Helping us mitigate the things that limit us.

Guiding us to be better.

Enjoy the journey. You won't regret it.

A.D. Detrick, President
MetriVerse Analytics

Iconography: Dan Haugen

ISBN: 9781795242073

1

INTRODUCTION

This makes sense for anything you care about

— JoAnne Weller (Greg's Mom)

In the early 2000s, I was a measurement consultant for a professional services company. This meant I advised clients about what they should measure (and how they should measure it) to gauge the success of a project, a department, or a whole company. It was to *my* company's benefit to keep me busy on billable projects because otherwise they were paying me while not making any money *from* me. This is bad in the professional services world. It's important to note here that while I was a consultant and had a role in helping win new customers, I wasn't a salesperson. The process of finding leads, contacting prospects, and closing sales wasn't my direct responsibility. The relevance of this distinction will be evident shortly.

One year, in response to increased revenue targets for

my department, the VP of sales asked me for my recommendations to meet those targets. I was glad he asked because a consultant with no billable work has a target on his back, and I liked my job. In preparation for the meeting, I had spent some time with our sales data and learned the sales conversion rate (the percentage of leads that become sales), the sales cycle time (how many days it takes to close a sale), and the average revenue per sale for the measurement practice. With the monthly revenue targets and a little Excel math, I used the conversion rate, cycle time, and average sales revenue to calculate how many dollars of measurement work needed to be in the sales pipeline (deals that are in process) each month to meet the sales quota.

The sales VP rolled his eyes a little at my calculations. His style was to lead by intuition (a.k.a. his gut), and he wasn't much interested in my analysis. His plan was to "shake things up" and change the kinds of business the company pursued in the first place. He was certain that this shake-up would be the path to huge success. He wasn't very clear on the new plan, but it seemed clear to him that *my* plan was bad.

Vision is critical to business success, but by choosing to ignore the historical successes (and failures) described in the data, he was shooting in the dark. We missed our revenue targets that year for the measurement practice, and that VP didn't make it through the second quarter before he was given the opportunity to take his vision elsewhere. Maybe there's no connection. Or maybe he missed an opportunity to pair my data to his vision to meet those revenue targets. We'll never know (although I have some suspicions).

A radical vision can be awesome, and many businesses are successful even when leaders ignore available data and take intuitive leaps. But intuition works most often when the data informs the leap. There were stories to be told in the sales data that might have helped form that VP's strategy—if in no other way than to direct him toward a path not traveled and encourage him to look for data from sources other than our own. There were also stories about where the leads were coming from, how to increase the conversion rate, or how to improve some other part of the existing process. But there were no KPIs that were useful to him besides end-of-month revenue. And the problem there was that once we missed the revenue for the month, it was too late to go back for a redo. The size of the pipeline, the conversion rate, and the sales cycle time were all enablers and early predictors of revenue success, and he missed the chance to use them that way.

How to Use This Book

The information in this book will help you measure and improve the performance in your job. This is the thing we're always doing, right? We're either trying to drive improvement in a stable environment, trying to remain consistent in a changing environment, or even scarier (and more common), trying to improve performance in a chaotic environment (you know who you are).

Definition: Performance

KPIs can be financial, operational, behavioral, customer satisfaction-al, or something entirely new and different. So "performance" will stand in for any and all of these (financial performance, operational performance, and so on). Performance is a statement of results compared to a goal, target, or standard. Whether the performance turns out to be good or bad depends on the target.

Case Studies - I've had the benefit of lots of learning experiences in my career (translation: failures—mine and other people's), and I want to share the great learning that comes from those experiences—particularly the failures. I'll indicate some of those case study examples with a folder icon.

Anecdotes - Throughout the book, I'll also share simplistic examples (often food related) about measuring success. It's easier to learn something new separate from its real-life context first. Those anecdotes will be marked with a notepad icon.

Definitions - There will also, predictably, be a number of terms and concepts that are open to interpretation. Rather than muck around in the various merits of the scholarly definitions of those words, I'll clarify how I'm using the terms *here*. Definitions will be marked with a dictionary icon.

Tips - When you want to jump ahead past the details, or if you just want a summary of the point I'm making, I'll show you tips and shortcuts to things and will indicate those tips with a lightbulb icon.

Success Coffee - Then, to provide context, we'll build a business (a coffee shop) of our own to make it all a little more real. I'll use the evolving case study of that coffee shop to illustrate each of the key points in the book, and those will be marked with a coffee icon.

The examples and methods I talk about here are not new. They have been used to measure success and improve performance for decades, probably longer. What's new is that I'm going to make it easy to understand and easy to do. You don't need a ton of supplies, a team of data analysts, or a degree. In almost all cases, you only need the math you learned as a kid, a pencil, and some paper. So relax and realize as you read that you knew this all along. In fact, you already do this every day.

This book will help you improve. Notice the period at the end of that sentence. The most obvious application of what you'll learn here will be in a business setting. The information and techniques here apply equally to your customer service organization, your manufacturing organization, your information technology organization, or your coffee shop (more on that shortly). It also applies to your home improvement project, your next vacation, or that book you've always wanted to write. If you were going to travel to an unknown location, you would use a map, and so will we. We'll start where you are now (literally or metaphorically) and identify where you want to go next—and then we'll make a plan for how to get there. This book will help you draw that map.

Who Are We?

So who am I? I've had an amazing career and have a lot still to go. Either I was drawn to process mapping and measurement because they matched my way of thinking, or I was impressionable when they were introduced. Either way, they remain the core of how I think. I worked in quality improvement for the first non-Japanese company to win the Deming Prize (an international award for quality control measures); I've been a consultant to manufacturing and service organizations in ISO

9000 quality control methods; I've measured and improved customer satisfaction in a number of different organizations; and I've spent a few years helping Fortune 100 companies measure the impact of their corporate learning strategies. In each case, before I ever opened a single spreadsheet, the conversation started with some version of "what's important to you?"

Because in all those cases, I found that time spent clarifying what was important led directly into what to measure: KPIs. Sometimes I made the mistake of jumping right to the data, believing that a numeric target and a mission were the same. They're not. And if you confuse the two, the metrics will get you pretty far down the wrong path before you realize you've lost track of your mission.

So who are you? You might sit—or want to sit—somewhere with a view of both the front line and the bottom line, meaning that you're close enough to see the sales, manufacturing, or service work and can also see the high-level revenue and cost measures. You might have a small organization that you want to grow into a big organization or at least a medium-sized one. You might have responsibility for a small part of a large organization or be responsible for bringing two organizations together. In short, if you have a goal you can imagine, this book is for you.

Let's Make This Easy

I think we sometimes make things more complicated than they need to be. In the case of KPIs, I think we make metrics and measurement more complicated than they need to be. This is because for some folks, math is fun! These folks (I'm occasionally one of these folks) get super excited about finding a new and complex statistical or financial model that some big brains have been talking about in nerdy math circles. While those models are great for finding reliable answers to complex problems, most of us find it impossible to start there.

TIP! KPIs 101

Mission—a thing you want to be true that isn't already true

Strategy—the ways you'll make that mission come true

Processes—the steps you'll take to pursue that strategy

Goals—the process outcome you're planning to achieve

Tactics—exactly what you'll do and by when

Improvements—how you'll analyze and improve performance

I know you're here for the KPI part, but I can't get you there until I get through these other parts because otherwise it won't make sense. Approaching your mission, strategies, and goals thoughtfully will ensure clarity in your organizational thinking. It will also prevent the rework that goes along with overlapping goals and unclear KPIs.

What Is a KPI?

TIP!
KPIs are what you pay attention to so you can gauge the health of something.

Key performance indicators (KPIs) are simply those things you pay attention to so you can gauge the health of something (like a project, department, or company) and in this context, health is success. They are those measures that, taken together, allow you to focus your effort on the best path to your mission. They *can* be complicated if you're into complicated data models, but I'm not. So I'm going to avoid complication in this book. There are operational KPIs and marketing KPIs and financial KPIs and a zillion other subcategories. But regardless of the category or subcategory, KPIs are what you measure to take action to increase revenue or decrease cost (or both). I'm going to let that simmer for a moment before saying it again. KPIs are what you *measure* in order to take *action* to increase revenue or decrease cost. Side note: the rules in non-profit and government organizations are sometimes not as focused on revenue and cost, but the approach is the same. Those organizations are also responsible for not spending more than they bring in.

There are KPIs, and then there are plain old performance indicators (although no one calls them PIs) that are subordinate to KPIs. In order to talk about KPIs, I need to talk about the subordinate performance indicators, too. Because non-key performance indicators are subordinate to KPIs, they predict the likely success of your KPIs.

The right KPIs are the ones that measure progress toward a specific mission—not just whatever measurement is available. Some organizations choose KPIs accidentally because they don't ask themselves the right questions—that is, the questions that lead to their mission. A mission is what you want to be true, and KPIs are how you know if you get there (with some other stuff in between). But if you're not careful, the KPI can become the mission itself (reduce cost, increase sales, reduce lost-time injury claims, reduce material waste), which is a mistake. If not attached directly to a larger mission—like "provide a safe work environment"—those are simply orphaned KPIs. An orphaned KPI is one that has lost its mission (very sad). Keeping your KPIs paired to a mission keeps you focused on your mission, strategy, and goals.

Definition: Key Performance Indicators (KPIs)

In the ocean of possible things to measure, some are more important, or "key," to success. Everything that gets done is a process. The measurable success of a process is the "performance." The "indicator" is the data itself.

It's important to remember that a KPI *represents* something rather than *being* the thing. For example, the numeric score on a customer satisfaction survey isn't actually the same as satisfaction, which is a nuanced human feeling. That score is an indicator of (or a pointer toward) satisfaction.

KPIs describe the health of an organization in the same way that a map describes a landscape. It's important that the map be as accurate as possible so travel is as predictable as possible, but there will always be differences in the reality that the map can't keep up with.

Why Bother with KPIs?

There are lots of people in business. Some run successful organizations without KPIs, or at least that's what they'll tell you. These folks will say that their instinct, or their gut, is the best indicator they have of whether to go left or go right. In some ways, I think that's true. Start-ups are notorious for living off of vision, gut reaction, and caffeine until they're viable. But those gut reactions are actually based on that person's awareness of key performance indicators. The person "leading with their gut" likely doesn't consider that they are leading with KPIs, when in fact gut reactions signify awareness of indicators about the state of a market, the potential of a customer base, or the future of an idea.

Here's how that goes: Super Awesome Gut Reaction Leader (SAGRL) has a company of two hundred people. She is carving out a new place for her company in a new market, so her decisions are quick and sometimes not intuitive to her employees. One morning on the news, SAGRL hears about growth in a different niche of this new market than the one she and her company are pursuing. Almost unconsciously, SAGRL evaluates the source of the report (degree of trustworthiness), how similar this new niche is to the one she's already pursuing (benchmark against current market), the growth potential (forecast of market forces), and the cost of shifting the direction of her company (awareness of her own profit and loss statement). For seasoned leaders, this kind of analysis can happen over a cup of coffee while they listen to the radio and hear the story. This gets called a gut reaction because nothing ever goes onto a piece of paper or a PowerPoint slide. But make no mistake—this was a quick analysis of internal KPIs used to make a decision. This kind of shorthand analysis is critical in any fast-moving team or organization, and the risk is that any of those internally made conclusions could be off, which would result in a failure of the desired outcome (in this case meeting an emerging need in the market). The good news is that small, agile organizations can usually pivot quickly to another scenario.

Visionaries are great, but when it's time for an organization to grow and scale, evidence-based decision-making provides more reliable results and allows other members of the organization to apply the same mission and goals to their work. KPIs allow you to assign measurable value to work and, I might argue, to your life as well. Whether it's a Tuesday and you're at the office or a Saturday and you're at home, there are a lot of things you *could* do. How will you pick the one you *will* do? How will you pick the one that will get you the greatest return? Through KPIs.

So What?

The most important question I've asked (and been asked) in a business setting is "To what end?" or stated more succinctly, "So what?" I'm glad you asked. The purpose of all these KPIs and all this measurement is to improve process performance. In some awesome situations, performance is already excellent, and KPIs help monitor and maintain that performance. But if you're like most of us, KPIs are expected to lead to actual improvements in results. So despite the prevalence of "just do better" or "just try harder" or some other vague platitude, your KPIs actually also hold the key to their own improvement.

Coffee, Anyone?

Missions are subjective expressions of who we want to be. And who we want to be right now are coffee shop owners (you didn't know, did you?). Strategies are how we accomplish the mission, and the day-to-day processes we engage in are how we develop and achieve goals to achieve those strategies. KPIs at every level bring it all together. There are successful businesses that don't have robust KPIs, but working like that doesn't make growth easy and makes problem-solving much tougher.

I drink a lot of coffee, and I sit in a lot of coffee shops. Although I live in a pretty coffee-intensive city, I suspect that you, wherever you live, have also bought a cup in a coffee shop. So throughout this book, I'm going to use the example of a coffee shop to illustrate my points. Don't worry—the details have been vetted by coffee shop professionals, so if you read this book in your local coffee shop, you won't feel like a fraud. In pursuit of a good self-fulfilling prophecy, we'll name it Success Coffee. And to fulfill that prophecy, I'll explore a mission, strategies, goals, processes, KPIs, and improvement ideas for Success Coffee.

2

MISSIONS AND STRATEGIES

Act the way you'd like to be, and soon you'll be the way you'd like to act.

— LEONARD COHEN

S uccess is relative. What's important to you won't be important to someone else, and what's important to you this year won't be important next year. This all starts with a mission: something you want to do that isn't already true.

~

Tip!
Success is relative.

Your mission is accomplished through your strategy, which is accomplished through your goals, which are met through improving processes. KPIs are what you measure throughout those layers. If your mission is the thirty-thousand-foot "what," your strategy is "how," and your goals are the ground-level "what."

Let's imagine your **mission** is to get healthy (a good mission). You might set one **strategy** to eat better and another strategy to exercise more. To accomplish that exercise strategy, you create a **process** for jogging a short distance every day with the **goal** to jog one mile by the end of the year. Your marathon-running neighbor, in comparison, might have a target to run a twenty-six-mile marathon this year. One approach is not better than the other—they might even be the same mission but with strategies, goals, and targets that define success differently for different circumstances. If you're successful at the one-mile jog, you might eventually run a marathon, but those would also be different circumstances.

Why are we starting with a touchy-feely mission instead of good solid data? Because KPIs are data presented in support of relatively arbitrary missions and goals. I've worked with organizations that debated which KPIs were the right ones (and sometimes ended up just using them all) for months and then then spent minutes deciding what their strategies and goals were. Those organizations did it backward. They identified the measures that seemed important and then allowed everything else to be the achievement of the measures.

The better approach starts with a mission: Who, where, or what do you want to *be*? And once you know who you want to be, the path to that is your strategy, and the distance you want to travel on that path is the goal. If you and I started a company making coffee cups, we could be makers of low-cost coffee cups, hand-crafted artisan coffee cups, or high-quality porcelain coffee cups. For each of those (and the endless other choices for what we might want our coffee cup company to be), there are different measures of success, which is to say, different KPIs that map directly to those missions.

~

Case Study: Billable Utilization

The primary KPI for an accounting firm I worked for was the billable utilization of its employees. Clients were charged a fixed amount each month based on the size of their business. If the bookkeeper estimated that closing the client's monthly books was a sixteen-hour job, that employee should bill sixteen hours. There was no incentive to complete sixteen hours of work in fourteen hours or to make recommendations for further work to the client.

Rather than a strategy of providing an array of financial services to these companies or of reducing the time to complete some tasks, the company lost strategic growth opportunities by focusing on bookkeeper utilization.

Who Do You Want to Be?

First you get yourself a mission and a strategy. Then you get yourself a goal and a process to meet that goal, and then finally you decide what to measure. Your mission is always an action statement (something you're going to do) in pursuit of something you want to be true that isn't currently true. If you're in a department of a larger organization, don't let the organizational mission stand in for your departmental or team mission. Obviously your team mission is subordinate to (and so needs to support) the overall mission, but you need to also have one for your team.

Definition: Missions and Visions

These are either exactly the same or very very different, depending on which expert you ask. I only refer to the mission here, though some will say that the mission is in pursuit of the vision. This isn't wrong (or exclusively right), but the distinction isn't necessary for this focus on KPIs.

Microsoft's mission statement is "to empower every person and every organization on the planet to achieve more." General Electric's mission statement is "to invent the next industrial era, to build, move, power, and cure the world," and the American Red Cross's mission statement is to "prevent and alleviate human suffering in the face of emergencies by mobilizing the power of volunteers and the generosity of donors."

Some of these are more marketing than truly aspirational (or truly measurable), but each of them provides key terms that point toward measurement. If you're Microsoft, you might seek measures of global access to technology—then within those measures, you might find access to technology by developing countries, creating a strategy of increasing empowerment in certain developing countries. That would be one way to make that mission measurable.

If you're GE, you might choose "build," "power," or "cure" and may also want to narrow down "the world" to something smaller that allows the development of a strategy (for example) aimed at power in a specific part of the world. If you're the Red Cross, you might, again, parse the mission and choose "alleviate human suffering in the face of emergencies" as a specific area for which to develop a strategy.

In all of these, a very broad, or macro, mission statement is broken down in order to create a subordinate strategy (or strategies). Strategies that are subordinate to a mission are critical to a KPI structure that drives your organization's (or department's) success. This reductionist focus on one part (often the largest contributor or the largest opportunity) of a larger whole is an effective way to drive the most change.

~

Anecdote: Nob

I once played a multiplayer online fantasy role-playing game. I chose *ranger* as my character, envisioning my virtual self fighting dragons, fighting bandits, fighting evil characters, and generally just fighting (ideally winning). I named my ranger Nob after an incredibly minor character in the Lord of the Rings.

Nothing came easily in this game. If I wanted a

sword, armor, or even pants, Nob the Ranger had to buy it. Nob the Ranger needed money. So he caught and sold fish to a market in town (this was an elaborate virtual world). Nob needed a lot of stuff, so he caught and sold a lot of fish. I logged into the game one day and was greeted as Nob the Fisherman. I was incensed. Dragons and bandits were never brought low by a fisherman.

The game had rightly measured the actions I was most consistently engaged in, and "Nob the Fisherman" was how I actually spent my time instead of how I thought I spent my time.

True, most industries and operations measure their success in similar ways. Manufacturing organizations measure throughput; retail organizations (brick-and-mortar ones) measure sales per square foot; and everyone is measuring margin and profitability. But what makes one group stand out in a sea of similarities is something unique: a different mission. Something that identifies who they want to be rather than who everyone else is. Missions can be set for an entire organization or for a program or department within that organization.

Start by clearly defining your mission in terms of a state of being—who you want to be or what you want to be true—rather than a number. You'll inspire the happiest customers in your industry. You'll provide the best parts to the best manufacturers. You'll serve a previously unexplored market segment. Each of these includes state-of-being words ("happiest," "best," "unexplored") that you will define when you develop your strategy. Your strategies for reaching that mission can change yearly, and your goals can change yearly, quarterly, or even monthly. But your mission should have some staying power.

As you identify what's important to you, you will by default identify some things that are *not* important or at least are *less* important to your mission. There are any number of different missions for your business or your department (or your life, for that matter) that you could pick. And if you're not very clear in the beginning about what's important to you, you will almost certainly end up measuring the wrong things. All of this sounds like a wide-open field of possibilities, and in many ways it is. But having said that the sky's the limit, let me make it easier. If your mission isn't somehow related to your customers (who provide the revenue that keeps you in business), you're making a mistake. Every successful organization gets there because they do what customers want and are willing to pay for. So as you're defining who you want to be, look for some statement of who you want to be *to your customers*.

With your mission in place, your strategies and goals stem from that mission and create focus for your work. You'll find that there are lots of things you want to be true —even lots of things that are important and lots of missions that bubble to the top of your thinking here. The exercise of creating your mission should seem a little like defining what kind of organization (or person) you want to be. Don't take this to mean that you have to reduce your mission; you don't. Do, however, think about how you'll make money with that mission. If you're creating a mission for an internal department, think about how you'll drive revenue or reduce costs within your department. But if you're in business, you likely want to *stay* in business, so your mission should point you to a strategy that reflects something that someone is willing to pay for.

Anecdote: Green Peppers

Imagine you and your neighbor each have an acre of land next door to each other, and you both plant green peppers. You both buy seeds, both till the soil, and both plant your seeds. Your neighbor buys the best weed control and pest control chemicals available for growing peppers. At the end of the season, she and her family harvest five hundred crates (twenty-five pounds each) of green peppers. After subtracting all her expenses, and after persuading her family to help harvest, she made a net profit of $5 per crate for a profit of $2,500. Those peppers go directly to a regional chain of Mexican restaurants for their menu. Fajitas!

Meanwhile, across the picket fence, you go a different way. Committed to organic food, you forego the chemicals and instead hire helpers throughout the season to manually pick weeds and apply gentle organic pest control. Your costs are higher for this reason, but you can ask a higher price for your green peppers because they're organic. At the end of the season, you also convince your family to help harvest and you get 312.5 crates of peppers (also twenty-five pounds each), and after subtracting your expenses, you also have a profit of $2,500.

Who was more successful? Both small farms made the same money at the end, though they got there in different ways. The answer, of course, is neither (from a financial perspective) and both (from a mission perspective). The definition of success has everything to do with the values of each farmer.

The Power of How

Company missions do a great job of highlighting what's important. The critical next question in response to "what" is "how." In fact, the act of asking "how" can build a path from the vaguest mission statement to a series of clear strategies.

Remember that Microsoft's mission was "to empower every person and every organization on the planet to achieve more." How could they do that? Choose "empower every person on the planet" or "empower every organization on the planet" or just "achieve more" and ask how. *How* could Microsoft empower every person on the planet to achieve more? This "how" is pretty broad, so let's assume that one view of "every person" includes people of all ages. How could they do that? With a strategy to develop software targeted to a broader age range of users. *How* could Microsoft target software to a broader range of users? Among other means, by documenting use cases for infant development through software. *How* could Microsoft document use cases for infant development? You see where this is going. Starting with an imprecise statement, we made choices about which direction to go, even though there were several possibilities at every "how." We could have similarly gone the route of seniors or people in developing countries (without easy access to software) or any other way of defining *all people on the planet.*

Case Study: Department Mission

The risk management department in a client company tracked about thirty different defects that were unrelated to each other. Hired to create order out of chaos, I did some interviews about why their department existed and what they thought would happen if their department disappeared. What would be the impact on the customers? On the company?

The consensus was that by reducing risk, this department was preventing risky products from getting to customers, thus preventing lawsuits. That quickly, I uncovered the department's mission: provide only safe products to customers and protect the company from lawsuits. KPIs strategies have been built on way less than that.

Their top-level KPI was the percentage of safe products in the hands of customers.

What You Want, Not What You're Avoiding

In the same way that it can seem easy for KPIs to replace missions, it can also seem easy to state your strategies or goals as things you're avoiding. For example, a goal to reduce customer complaints is too limiting. Choose instead to increase customer satisfaction—even if you measure it by a reduction in complaints (which has its own problems but isn't a terrible measure). The key to your mission is that it is what you *want*, not what you're trying to avoid. This book is about measuring success, not counting failures. (That's usually too easy, and there are already plenty of books about how to stop doing things that are unpleasant.)

As an example, many manufacturing organizations where people work with machinery will have a lost-time injuries KPI. These are injuries that result in an employee having to take time away from work. Lost-time injuries is a commonly used KPI, and reducing such a KPI is always good. But as a mission, "reducing lost-time injuries" is a statement of avoidance, not forward motion. If your mission says that you value employees, your strategy could be that you create a safe workplace and measure it by lost-time injuries. Is it clear? It is. Is it measurable?

Absolutely. Is it achievable? For the sake of the employees, I hope so.

Let's Open a Coffee Shop, Shall We?

I worked in restaurants for thirteen years, including providing strategic consulting for a restaurant chain, so building a coffee shop throughout this book was pretty exciting for me. Let's assume we're opening this coffee shop together and that this begins our series of conversations about who we want to be. For Success Coffee, there are (as there always are) choices for our mission:

Shop 1. High-volume mid-cost coffee drinks for the masses. We will compete with the big coffee chains with a model that will be able to scale to any size. Customers will have a predictable experience when they come in. We won't be the coffee shop where they'll want to sit and hang out with friends, lingering over a latte for two hours. Our mission: we offer consistently good coffee and muffins at a reasonable price.

Shop 2. Drip coffee and prepackaged muffins at a discount. We'll be half the price of the big chains because we'll be mostly self-service. Customers will come in, pay at the register, serve themselves a cup of drip coffee, add cream and sugar if they want, and buy a prepackaged pastry if they want. For a couple of bucks, they'll leave quickly with a decent start to their day. Customers who don't need all that highbrow espresso will love our simple brew. Our mission: we offer consistent-tasting coffee and muffins for budget-conscious customers.

Shop 3. Low-volume artisan coffee. Not just a cup of coffee—this is a coffee experience. Single-origin organic beans, precision ground, experimental brewing methods, and highly trained staff will create the connoisseur's cup of coffee. Our customers will be a select group whose standards are high, or they'll be people who want to learn how to set higher standards for themselves. Our mission: we educate our customers about the best-tasting coffee by only offering the best.

Shop 4. An approachable cut above. High-quality espresso drinks and freshly made muffins served by friendly, knowledgeable staff. Our customers may not drive across town (and past a dozen other cafés) because we're better than all the others, but they'll come because we're in their neighborhood and we're good. Our mission: Hey we build community by offering fresh-baked muffins and fresh-roasted espresso drinks in our neighborhood.

∿

Case Study: The Best Restaurant

I once worked for one of the most popular restaurants in town, known for the quality of its food. Salad dressings were homemade, cream was whipped fresh for every dessert, and fried cheese was breaded by hand and served with homemade marinara sauce. Customers were willing to pay a little more for a special meal, and the restaurant prospered until the owners sold the business.

The new owners kept prices high but lowered costs by (among other changes) getting salad dressings, whipped toppings, and cheese sticks delivered in bulk. By trying to be both a high-price destination and low-cost eatery, they failed at both. Three years after the sale, the restaurant closed.

Our Mission

Starting with "let's open a coffee shop" may have seemed clear, but who we *become* has everything to do with who we *want* to become. I've seen countless businesses stumble when they couldn't decide between (for example) being the low-cost provider and the specialty provider. Both have their niche and their customers, but it's tough for one business to do both well, so we'll pick just one.

In our high-volume, mid-cost coffee shop (Shop 1), how would we set a strategy and goals for that mission? We'd look for deals on midgrade coffee and pastries and drive consistent processes so our coffee is always at the same roast, same temperature, and same coffee-to-milk ratio regardless of who's making it. In our low-volume artisan coffee shop (Shop 3), how would we realize that mission? We'd find the best coffee and the best pastries from the finest ingredients, and our staff would be thoroughly trained to be more coffee consultants than baristas. And of course, our prices would reflect the higher value (and the higher cost).

There are lots of successful coffee shops and lots of different ways of getting there. For the sake of this book, we'll go with Shop 4, and our mission will be to "build community by offering fresh-baked muffins and fresh-roasted espresso drinks in our neighborhood."

How will we realize that mission? Our strategy will include definitions of "fresh" for both muffins and for coffee as well as a definition for "community" so we can develop goals to support it. A full KPI structure looks like the expanding root system of a tree (where the trunk is the mission) because the mission will have multiple strategies, and each strategy will have multiple processes with multiple goals. Even for a small coffee shop, there is a lot to unpack in our mission.

Though it's not a stated part of our mission, it's implied that we need revenue and cost strategies because we've got to make more money than we spend. I'll dig more deeply into financial measures and KPIs, but the short version is that gross margin—the percentage of what we make that we don't have to pay in costs—is our highest-level financial measure. Financial measures stand quietly, holding the signs and adjusting the microphone for the more charismatic missions. But they know, as the missions do, that unless we're financially solid, the mission won't get us anywhere.

Success Coffee mission: We build community by offering fresh-baked muffins and fresh-roasted espresso drinks in our neighborhood.

3

PROCESSES

If you can't describe what you're doing as a process, you don't know what you're doing.

— W. Edwards Deming

Processes

The first thing to know about process is that all processes in an organization should either drive revenue *in* or drive cost *out*. In some cases, the connections are simple (the sales process drives revenue in), and in some cases, the connections are more complex (customer service can enable repeat revenue and can also drive down escalation costs). The more complex the organization, the tougher it can be to see the connection to financial measures, but they're there.

The next thing to know about process is that all work can be defined as a process, and all success is measured by the performance of those processes. I'm going to pause here because a lot happened in that sentence, and I want to make sure it didn't happen too quickly. *All* work (and all play and all rest) is a process. A process is simply a series of steps that are usually completed in some order and that result in a specific outcome. You work in processes all the time and may not even realize it. That is to say, first you do one thing, then you do another, and then you do another. The successful outcome of a process *is* its success measure.

Definition: Subordinate Processes

One of the most common measures of customer service in call centers is average handle time (AHT). AHT is a measure of all the things that happen between when the call connects and when the call disconnects (that's the process). The key to understanding unexpected changes in AHT and how to improve it is understanding the component parts like talk time, hold time, and after-call work (subordinate processes).

Each of your processes is made up of subordinate processes (which have their own subordinate processes), and each of those have their own success measures. You will see that one or more of those subordinate processes make a greater contribution to your overall process success than others. Based on each of their relative contributions to the main process measure, they will point the way to picking the lowest-hanging fruit.

Nearly any process can be broken down into subordinate processes. The process of making breakfast might include baking blueberry muffins, scrambling eggs, and making coffee. In the overall process of preparing breakfast, the muffins, the eggs, and the coffee are all subordinate processes that have their own subordinate steps. Baking blueberry muffins is a process comprising the subordinate processes of cracking an egg, measuring flour, and mixing batter. Each of those subordinate processes has its own steps and success measures, as does the overall muffin-making process. I'll talk about processes at strategic and tactical levels to show how to build a bridge between the actions you can take and the impact on your financials.

TIP!
Measuring Success: Thing + specification + time = success.

Because processes have subordinate processes, the choice of what process outcome to measure isn't always clear and will likely require thought, if not collaboration. There are some guiding principles to consider, such as which sub-process takes the most time (or most other resources), or which sub-process is most critical (one could argue that blueberry muffins aren't critical). The point is that these are not necessarily clearly defined and so will need to be defined before developing your KPIs.

The formula for process success is **thing + specification + time = success**. *Thing* is the expected outcome of the process. Cookies are the "thing" for a cookie-baking process. Arriving at work is the "thing" for the process of going to work. *Specification* defines the specifics of the thing, also often called "quality," which usually translates to the customer expectations. Cookies that are crumbly or squishy or chocolatey are examples of thing + specification. Finally, *time*, which is the thing we can't ever get more of (unless the sci-fi writers have been right all this time), captures whether the thing was delivered when it was needed or expected. So everyone is working to get their thing at their specification and in the right time. Your organization is too.

This chapter is about processes, and the next one is about goals. Separating goals and processes is a bit arbitrary since goals are the successful outcomes of processes.

But there is enough to say about processes that I wanted to give them their own chapter. The work we do, the play we engage in, the food we cook, the way we sleep, and so on are all processes that happen in good old linear time. They all also have successful outcomes and failed outcomes (or defects) from which KPIs come. If the outcome is the "what," then the process is the "how."

You may be used to hearing about process, process mapping, process analysis, and process measurement as if it's a technical science. Nothing could be further from the truth (though like anything else, the deeper you go, the more sciencey it can get). But let's start at the version of process mapping that you do every day.

Processes and Sub-processes

A fractal is an awesome blend of nature and mathematics. It describes (among other things) a geometric pattern where greater detail is revealed at increasingly small scales than is visible at a larger scale. One classic fractal example is a snowflake, which has the same structural pattern whether viewed with the naked eye or under a magnifying glass.

Processes and sub-processes are like that. Whatever process you're looking at can be broken down into smaller sub-processes. Then each of those sub-processes can be broken down into further sub-sub-processes and so on. And of course, the original process you started with is a sub-process if looked at from a different point of view.

≈

Anecdote: Fractals

Benoît Mandelbrot was a mathematician who observed in the 1960s that the measured length of a coastline (in this case, Britain) varied depending on the scale. If measured in centimeters, more detail was visible, resulting in a longer measured result than if the same stretch of coastline had been measured in meters. This is because the centimeter stick could more closely adhere to the detail (the curves) of the coastline than the meter stick would. The extrapolation of this finding describes an increasing (and limitless) measure of surface area as the scale approached zero. Mandelbrot was the first to use the term "fractal" in describing a pattern that repeats at different scales.

There's a whole process (at least for me) in getting ready to go to work in the morning. Steps in that process include getting up, getting coffee, getting dressed, and getting out the door. All those together are the process for going to work. Getting dressed is simultaneously its own process and is a sub-process within the getting ready for work process. This means every process you can map is made up of shorter sub-processes (which are also made up of shorter sub-processes). Your mind just expanded a little, I know.

Because of all this macro- and micro-process mapping, the decision about where a process starts and ends is a bit arbitrary. Does getting ready for work include having breakfast, or is that a different process? Yes and no. It's not important that I decide here (or even that we agree), but it *is* important that *you* decide. In manufacturing, the process of making a ball bearing starts with stamping the steel. Or it may start earlier at the materials delivery or even earlier when the original steel is smelted. So a process may be long, with many sub-processes, or it may be short and focused, depending on which view allows you to take the best action for improvement.

A Word About Time

Processes happen in time, which is to say we do one thing, then another thing, then a third thing. If the process is cooking, we add the ingredients, *then* we stir the dough, *then* we bake the cookies, *then* we pour the milk, *then* we eat. Each of these steps takes a second or a minute or an hour, and *between* the things, there is also a second or a minute or an hour. All those steps and in-betweens add up to the time it takes to complete a process. See? Linear time, linear process. Sometimes the order of things can be mixed up (add salt before you add sugar, or add sugar first), but in a surprising number of processes, there is a single best order.

Organizations are no different. If the outcome you're seeking is more sales (the *what*), the place to drive that change is the sales process (the *how*). That is to say, first getting a lead, then calling that lead, then negotiating a deal, then closing a sale. Each of those steps takes time and has its own success measure. The foundation of measuring success, as I've said, is *defining* success, and that's best done through the lens of a process outcome. Let's start simple by mapping a process.

As you start to measure KPIs, you'll probably find yourself making arbitrary separations between your data, like things that happen on *this* day compared to things that happen on *that* day. In practice, data bleeds over from one time frame to another (transactions started on a Monday may continue into Tuesday), and the closer you look, the more you realize that the decision to report at the hourly, daily, weekly, monthly, or even yearly separation may be arbitrary, and the choice to look at a week or a rolling six weeks may tell a very different story. Tell the story that best describes where you want to go.

Mapping a Process

Process mapping is as complicated or as easy as you want it to be. But if you've been here this long, you know I'm going to make it easy. If you've ever made a list of errands to accomplish in a particular order, you've mapped a process. In fact, let's start that way and make a shopping list for a dinner party (shopping is a process). Assume you'll need at least ten different items from the grocery store, and just jot them down onto a list. If you went to the store and followed your list as it's written, you would be moving from location to location (from step to step) in the order you wrote them down and putting those items in your cart. Just like that, you've mapped a process.

Shopping: A Simple List for a Weird Dinner Party

- Celery
- Shredded cheese
- Sausage
- Crusty bread
- Toothpicks
- Cantaloupe
- Garlic
- Oranges
- Paper plates and napkins
- Canned tomatoes

This shopping experience is likely not an *efficient* process, but it's a process. You have identified steps that are executed in time and take some amount of time: both the step itself (taking an item off the shelf and putting it in your cart) and the time in between steps when you're wheeling your cart around.

An Ordered List

Once you've mastered list-making (which you likely mastered long ago), the next step is an ordered list—that is, a list of steps where the order matters. Do this by creating a list where some steps are dependent on other steps being done first. For example, if you want to ship a stuffed duck to a friend (I'm sure that's a thing people do), you need to first get a box, then put the duck in it, then seal the box, then address it, then add postage. True, some of those things can be done in different order, but the duck needs to go into the box before you seal it, or that duck isn't going anywhere.

Shipping a Duck: An Ordered List

1. Secure the duck.
2. Get the box.
3. Put the duck in the box.
4. Seal the box.
5. Address the box.
6. Add postage.

A Branching Ordered List

I'm using this simple example to illustrate a point, but as you can imagine, lists and ordered lists will get quite complicated when they involve multiple people or multiple departments. In your ordered list, as in most processes, there are also decision points where the list may branch in one or more different directions.

Shipping a Duck: A Branching Ordered List

Main Process

1. Secure the duck.
2. (Branch) Is the duck stuffed or live?
3. If stuffed, proceed to step 3.

4. If live, proceed to sub-process A.
5. Get the box.
6. Put the duck in the box.
7. Seal the box.
8. Address the box.
9. Add postage.

Shipping a Duck—Sub-process A

1. Read postage prohibitions for shipping live poultry.
2. Be kinder to living ducks.
3. Secure a stuffed duck.
4. Continue to main process step 3.

Despite the simplicity, this works exactly the same for all levels of complexity in process mapping. List the first thing, then the next thing, then the next thing. When there is a choice or decision point, list the steps for all possible branches. If you need to know more about an existing process, ask someone to walk you step by step through a process they perform. Very often the work to be done in process mapping for existing processes is evaluating whether the steps are still relevant and still add specific value to the overall outcome. In my above example, while being kinder to living ducks (sub-process A, step 2) is absolutely a good practice, it doesn't add value to the overall process of shipping a stuffed duck.

Developing a process for the first time takes a little more creativity and requires that you start with a desired outcome (the "thing" in the success formula) and ask yourself a series of "how" questions to see what it will take to get there. When you create a process this way, your "what" is the successful outcome of a series of steps and your "how" is the order in which you complete them. You do this all the time without thinking of it, and that skill extends easily to a business situation. Once you know what the success measure is, the best way to ensure success is to look back at the process to see whether the individual steps are aligned to the outcome.

Thing + Specification + Time = Success

You've created a list, an ordered list, and a branching ordered list. All these are the building blocks of mapping a process, so now let's add the most critical element: a success measure. The success measure for a process is often obvious. A software sales process should result in software sales, a widget manufacturing process should result in widgets, and an ATM withdrawal process should result in cash from the ATM.

In these examples, and in pretty much every other example, process improvement seeks to improve the success measure by altering the steps of the process. Let's start (as always) simply and with food. Specifically, let's start with the measurable outcome of a sandwich.

Long before anyone added sea salt to chocolate, peanut butter and jelly was the original salty and sweet flavor combination. If you don't know how to make a peanut butter and jelly sandwich, you will in a moment.

The process is as follows:

1. Take some bread out of the bag.
2. Get the peanut butter out of the cupboard.

3. Get the jelly out of the refrigerator.

4. Using a knife or a spoon (I often use a spoon), spread some peanut butter on one slice of bread.

5. Using a knife or spoon, spread some jelly on the other slice of bread.

6. Press the pieces of bread (peanut butter facing jelly) together.

7. (Optional but recommended) Cut the sandwich in half.

There it is: a documented process for achieving the measurable outcome of one sandwich (the "thing"). You'll find in nearly every situation that you need one or more qualifiers on an outcome to define what constitutes success, however. The sandwich itself is only the beginning. There is also room for greater specifics in the success measure (the "specification"):

- A sandwich with a specific calorie count
- A sandwich that doesn't drip jelly
- A sandwich with a specific peanut butter to jelly ratio

Each of these adds specificity to the definition of success. I said already that success is relative, and you learned what was important in creating a mission by understanding the unique needs of your unique customers. From those unique needs, you set the definition of success for *this* particular peanut butter and jelly sandwich. In many organizations, the measure of quality (including capital-Q Quality) isn't whether the thing exists but whether it exists *and* meets the specification. For this reason, specification is often labeled "quality," though without a clear definition, the word "quality" as a standalone description is like the word "temperature"— which is to say, not at all helpful.

Continuing the peanut butter and jelly example, each of those major steps (e.g., take the bread out of the bag) can be more precise. Take "some bread" becomes more precise (for this sandwich) to say, "two slices of bread" or even "two slices of one-hundred-calorie bread." Similarly, step 4 says "some peanut butter," and to be more precise, it could say "two tablespoons of peanut butter." This is the beginning of establishing specifications within your process. These specifications within the process also become the first of your enabling indicators—those measures that enable your final successful outcome.

And if we then add our old friend *time* (who will not be ignored) into the equation, we get a success measure of thing + specification + time = success. A peanut butter and jelly sandwich (thing) that doesn't drip (specification) and is ready in under five minutes (time). Or a sale of product X (thing) at full price (specification) in under thirty days from lead to close (time). Or a ball bearing no heavier than 5.35 grams manufactured in under seventy seconds. As you find (or map) the processes in your organization, look for (or create) success measures that combine those three components.

So we started with a list, then moved on to an ordered list and a process for making a sandwich. I talked about success measures as the desired outcome of the process.

These outcomes have been a shopping trip, a duck in a box, and a peanut butter and jelly sandwich. As I mentioned earlier, success is relative, and I talked about finding your mission because if you start with your destination, mapping the path is easier.

Now I want to talk about failed outcomes or defects. The word "defect" comes, as much of what we do in business does, from manufacturing. If I'm a cobbler and make shoes every day, I say a successful shoe holds together when a customer puts it on (it's a low bar in my cobbler shop). A defect is a shoe that comes apart at the seams when a customer puts it on. If I measure the number of successful shoes as a percentage of all the shoes I make (good shoes / good shoes + bad shoes), I have a success measure and a defect rate as well.

For most of your purposes, a defect will simply be an output of your process that doesn't meet your specifications. By simple definition, everything that is not a success is a defect, though in some processes there is a category for "in process" that allows accounting for all the materials and effort, even though some of the outcomes aren't complete yet. But you should expect that your outcomes are either successes or defects.

Stuff Is Made Up of Other Stuff

Core to your KPI strategy is understanding that stuff is made up of other stuff. A sandwich is a complete outcome in itself and is also made up of peanut butter and jelly and bread. The bread is its own complete outcome and is the result of a process that includes mixing flour and water and yeast, and even that flour comes from a process including wheat and (it turns out) niacin and other complicated-sounding preservatives. Saying stuff is made up of other stuff means we can go deeper and deeper into what things are made of. Similarly, if we go "up" from our sandwich, it is one part of a process called lunch. Lunch is a sandwich and chips and lemonade, and lunch is also part of a process of consuming one day's calories (including breakfast and dinner).

If I may also use a rare (for me) sports analogy, a baseball game is made up of (among other things) runs, while a baseball season is made up of baseball games. When team A gets more runs in a game than team B, the winner is team A. At the point that team B has lost, it's too late to prevent the loss. So there are all kinds of things that are tracked *during* the game (before win or loss is called), like getting base hits. If team B can focus in the middle of the game on getting more base hits, they can increase their likelihood of a win. In this case, base hits are an enabling indicator and predictive of winning, which is the KPI: the measure of success.

Because a baseball season is made up of baseball games (because stuff is made up of other stuff), let's expand this to a season. If team B loses the game to team A, it's too late to go back and win that game, but that loss may be an enabling indicator that allows them to change tactics and do better for the season overall.

KPIs are also sometimes referred to as lagging indicators, or indicators that lag behind the performance of the overall process. Enabling indicators are also knowns as leading indicators, which are those measured before the process end (they lead the final outcome). Similarly, KPIs are often known as lagging indicators because they lag behind the process steps.

Success Coffee Processes

Remember that our mission is "we build community by offering fresh-baked muffins and fresh-roasted espresso drinks in our neighborhood," and one of our strategies (specifically in support of "high-quality espresso drinks") is to "use only fresh-roasted coffee and fresh milk to craft perfect espresso drinks." There are tons of goals that can come from that strategy and our community mission, but we're focused just on espresso so far. And even though Success Coffee is a small business, there are lots of processes, so that's why we need to start with a goal.

Perfect espresso drinks—I'll assume we already have a good-quality grinder and espresso machine, though it's good to be sure about something that important. Remember that where we draw the line between processes is arbitrary, so let's decide, since great outputs start with great inputs, that this process starts with buying coffee beans and ends with handing the drink to the customer. (We could, of course, map the process for *finding* a good-quality coffee supplier as the first step. But we won't because boundaries.)

So we start with an ordered list as our overall process:

1. Order beans from supplier.
2. Pour beans in the grinder.
3. Grind coffee for each drink.
4. Pull espresso shot (coffee shop lingo, there).
5. Steam milk, if needed.
6. Prepare cup (paper or porcelain).
7. Hand coffee to customer.

Each of these processes is, of course, its own sub-process with its own success measures (and its own even deeper sub-processes). For example, achieving good-quality coffee relies on making good espresso between five and eight days of those beans being roasted. So the success measure for the ordering sub-process is receiving the coffee at the shop within four days of roasting, which means the enabling indicators for the ordering sub-process include the day the order is placed.

Now you've got a mission, you've got a strategy, and you've identified the key processes for how you'll achieve that strategy.

4

GOALS

What you get by achieving your goals is not as important as what you become by achieving your goals.

— Zig Ziglar

Your mission is what you want, your strategy is the path you'll take, your processes are the vehicle, and your goal is the outcome. As we did with the Microsoft and General Electric mission statements, you'll parse your mission into (usually) a series of strategies for which you need to set goals (including numeric targets).

One of the most common methods for goal setting (and one that works just fine so I won't try to retool it) is setting SMART goals. SMART is an acronym for specific, measurable, achievable, relevant, time bound.

- **Specific**—Be precise. "Grow in new market

segments" is too vague. Which market segments? Grow which parts of your business?

- **Measurable**—This refers to the ability to count how often the goal is met.
- **Achievable**—Goals are motivating if they're perceived to be achievable and also if they are a welcome challenge. There is a constant balance between challenging and easy.
- **Relevant**—Relevant to the business is good, but relevant to the day-to-day work of the people pursuing the goal is better.
- **Time bound**—This refers to the specific moment at which the goal is defined as reached or missed.

TIP! Strategy or Goal?
In a smaller organization or in support of a very specific mission, strategies and goals may merge. It's more important to have an actionable bridge between your mission and the action you take to achieve it than to worry about whether it's called a strategy or a goal.

What About Customers?

Let's talk about goals in terms of customers. If thing + specification + time = success, the definitions of each of those come through collaboration between the organization and the customer. Within an organization, contributors to this formula are usually called *stakeholders*, meaning anyone who could reasonably be expected to be annoyed if the goal isn't met. There are lots of reasons to involve stakeholders in defining what success means for your process or project, and the biggest reason is that success is always subjective. Different people value different things, and the time to find out that you and your boss have different success measures is *not* when the project has launched.

The easiest way to know whether your customers like your product or service is whether they pay for it. Subsets of "pay for it" include obviously "buy it," "buy it again" (repeat customers), "use it" (product adoption, subscription renewal), and "recommend it" (customer satisfaction, Net Promoter Score). Prior to knowing whether customers are willing to give you money for your work, there are both direct (focus groups, surveys) and indirect ways (people paying for similar products and services) to get their input.

That said, there are some who believe that asking customers what they want stifles innovation. There is a quote (inconclusively) attributed to Henry Ford: "If I had asked people what they wanted, they would have said faster horses." Whether Ford said it or not, it's a great description of a decision to innovate beyond customers' current expectations. Similarly, Apple doesn't do market research. I can confirm, from some consulting I did at Apple, that there has historically been a conscious decision not to do market research. The point isn't that these organizations aren't interested in their customers—quite the opposite. The difference is that they seek what customers *will* want rather than what they *do* want. This is a riskier approach because the gamble definitely misses more often than it hits (hello, Google Glass, which some say customers just haven't caught up to yet). My point is that the choice to innovate without customer input doesn't take customers out of the picture; it's instead a choice to believe that you know better than market research does. Whether fueled by direct customer input or not, deciding the best goal to support your strategy just requires some context.

What to Measure

Here's the best news I have for you today: everything is measurable. You're immediately skeptical, and I totally get that. True, not all measurement will have the same degree of precision, but I haven't yet come up with a situation I can't measure. People who want to measure something often believe that the choices are to know nothing (usually where they start) or know everything (which is rarely possible). So in the absence of knowing everything, those people will choose nothing and will say something isn't measurable. So if I can't know precisely how much money it will take to open a coffee shop, I can't possibly open a coffee shop. Except that I *can* make assumptions about things, assign values to those assumptions, and then add up those values. While those values might not have the accuracy that hindsight will provide about what something *actually* costs, I definitely have a closer version than nothing.

Anecdote: Enabling Indicators

Coal mining has always been a dangerous job. For a time, coal miners (in a smart move for coal miners but a tragic experience for canaries) would take a caged canary down into the mine with them as an enabling indicator (it's unlikely they used that term). Carbon monoxide, methane, or any other poisonous gas would kill the canary before it killed the coal miners, so a deceased canary was a warning to get out of the mine.

Once you've determined what's important and defined the processes and sub-processes, you need to figure out what to count (and under what circumstances) to measure your success. The thing you'll probably count at the top is money: the amount coming in and the amount going out. After that you'll be counting the frequency with which the processes in your organization have successful outcomes. You'll have work to do to define "successful outcome" for some processes, but for most of them, it'll be obvious. If you're in a nonprofit, or if you're in the middle of a larger organization, money may not be at the top for you, and something will stand in for the highest-level success of your department or organization.

Once you know your processes, your KPIs are the success measures for the highest-level processes, and the success measures for each of your sub-processes are your enabling indicators. Enabling indicators are your coal mine canaries, indicating the likelihood of your overall process having a successful outcome.

The measurable outcomes of those processes—your KPIs—are going to be made up of some kind of data, most likely quantitative (numerical) data rather than qualitative (descriptive). I'll talk a little bit about using statistics to tell the stories that are in complex data sets, and there are new financial and data models being built every day to get even more precision into business. But for our purposes, and to get you to something actionable, measurement is just counting; and if you've decided what goal supports your strategy, what you measure should simply be the frequency with which you meet that goal.

To get to the measurement part, you'll either not have the data you need or (more commonly) have *way* more data than you need, and you'll have to sort through it to find the right measure. In either case, measuring is just counting, and if there isn't strong data in place, I'll give you some things you can do to get directional data to get you started. Remember, everything is measurable.

Target Setting

With an aspirational mission and a well-crafted strategy, you now need a goal with a challenging but achievable target to bridge the gap between your current state and your desired state.

Case Study: Customer Service Quality

Once, when I was leading the quality team for a telecom provider, my boss popped into my office and asked how much I thought we could improve our J. D. Power customer service rating in the new year.

I guessed that if we could fix some persistent problems, we might get a 7 percent to 10 percent improvement and offered to dig into the data for a better answer. She said that was fine and left. The next week, I saw a company-wide announcement of our commitment to a 10 percent improvement in our J. D. Power scores. When I asked, she confirmed that she had taken my off-the-cuff response and presented it as a plan.

Predictably, we missed that target that year, and I

spent time in the latter part of the year analyzing the miss.

Target setting is often random, but it doesn't have to be. Many organizations, to make it easy, will take an educated-guess approach and ask for a percent reduction each year. This may take the form of a 5 percent reduction in costs, a 10 percent improvement in customer satisfaction, or a 15 percent increase in sales (educated-guess targets are often divisible by five). In my experience, this often means spending the middle and end of the year explaining why targets were exceeded early (not aggressive enough) or why they were missed (too aggressive or insufficient action taken).

Your approach to target setting should always seek a balance between meaningful improvement and the capability of the process itself. Meaningful improvement often boils down to improvement you can see or (often more importantly) improvement you can show someone else or improvement that matters to your customers. Some improvements seem meaningful (e.g., $10,000 saved) until looked at in context (e.g., $10,000 saved from a multimillion-dollar spend). For that reason many organizations reach for very large performance changes right out of the gate and are disappointed when they miss those targets because they are unwilling (or unable) to make the very large process improvements required to meet aggressive targets. Conversely, if targets are set too meekly, there will be many side-glances about how easy it is to achieve when expectations are low.

Anecdote: Process Capability

Every morning you walk a half mile to work at Success Coffee, noting the time you leave and the time you get there. After a few months, you calculate that the average (or mean) time to get to work is eighteen minutes. You also see that sometimes you're there in only fifteen minutes, and sometimes it takes as long as twenty-one minutes (that's the range).

If your process hasn't had a significant change, and you take the same route to work, wear similar walking shoes, and your walking pace is consistent, your arrival times will fall within a relatively tight range around that average. However, if you take a different route every day or frequently change the kind of shoes you wear, the range of travel times will vary more widely.

If you want to spend less time explaining why you missed your targets, set them based on the capability of the process. Process outcomes vary—even in precision environments and definitely in non-precision environments. Whether you're tracking ball bearing manufacturing, the mileage in your car, or the time it takes you to walk a mile, there will be some degree of variation between the outcomes. The ball bearing diameter will vary in tiny fractions of millimeters, the car mileage in single- or double-digit mileage, and the walk time will vary in minutes and seconds. That said, a process that hasn't had significant change for some time will usually perform consistently. That is to say, if you track the performance over time, it will vary—but within a predictable range. Targets set within that predictable range are within the process capability, and that target simply predicts future process performance based on past performance.

In order to effectively use past performance for target setting, you'll want a stable process that has performed within a predictable range for some time. "Some time" is relative: If yours is a manufacturing process that runs hundreds of times per hour, you might only need a few days of consistent variability to set targets. If yours is a monthly financial measure for a complex business, you may want more than a year of stability before setting target-based goals on process capability. In either case, once performance is relatively predictable, target setting could be (for example) taking the best performance from a previous time frame (last year, last quarter) and setting the target to be consistently achieving that performance or better. Consider the margin percentage chart below.

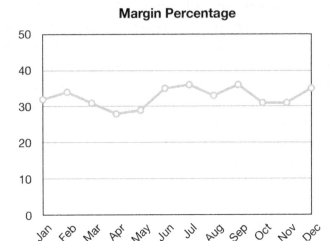

Margin Percentage

In the twelve-month margin history, the highest performance is 36 percent, and the lowest is 26 percent. A 30 percent target in the coming year is probably too meek since the margin has consistently been above that in the latter half of the year. Similarly, a target of 45 percent is probably too aggressive since the margin has never been that high and that target would require significant change in the way work is done (which may be a great idea if the organization is ready for that significant change). Finding the balance between what's possible and what's meaningful is an ongoing effort. You can measure how much that balance is off by how much time you spend explaining why you achieved your goal so easily (leaning toward what's possible) or why you missed it by such a large degree (leaning toward what's meaningful).

Statistical Capability

While rare outside of a precision manufacturing process, statistical capability is still useful to know about as a concept. I said already that targets set within the past performance range of relatively stable processes will meet the needs of many non-precision environments, and that's true. In the statistical version of that approach, the performance variation of a stable process is calculated mathematically as an expression of the performance variation compared to the average performance. "Stable" in this case is a process that performs consistently within six standard deviations of the average performance. Side note—*sigma* is the statistical term for standard deviation. The discipline of Six Sigma is named for a statistically stable process. This bit of trivia will be sure to impress at your next meeting.

Definition: Six Sigma

Six Sigma is a popular data-driven process improvement methodology. Sigma is another name for standard deviation, and Six Sigma refers to three standard deviations both above and below the average in a population. In a normal distribution, more than 99 percent of occurrences happen within those limits.

The below update on the margin percentage chart shows the same performance as before and now includes an average (AVG) line, an upper control limit (UCL), and a lower control limit (LCL). With these additional calculations, it's easy to see that all of the performance points fall between the upper and lower control limits, meaning this is a stable process. Targets set within those control limits are within the normal variability (and therefore the statistical capability) of the process—even if sustaining higher-than-average performance will still require some effort.

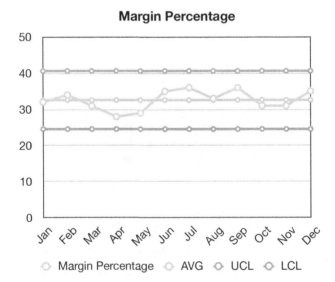

Setting a target between the upper and lower control limits means that the process historically (and currently) has the capability to achieve that target, and it's likely that some incremental improvement in the process will get you there. If you set a target outside of the upper and lower control limits, achieving it will require comprehensive change in your process itself.

Manufacturing organizations often use statistical control to continually refine and improve their processes, but in practice most other organizations don't track process performance like this. What *is* relevant and useful is having an understanding of whether your target can be achieved by incremental changes or whether you'll need a comprehensive process change. When a target is proposed that is not within the existing process capability (statistically or just historically), it becomes someone's job (yours, likely) to ask about the plan to change the process, since that sustained target isn't possible within the parameters of the existing process. The win in this conversation is to get agreement on either achievable targets or (even better) the need for significant process change—not just "go faster" or something equally non-helpful.

Goals are the mileposts on this journey. Sometimes missing them can be just as useful on the journey as achieving them. In either case, there's something good to learn.

5

BUILDING A KPI MAP

The map is not the territory

— ALFRED KORZYBSKI

Previously, in Measuring Success

Everything is a process, processes have successful outcomes (and defects), and the measure of process success is the goal in support of the strategy in support of the mission. The process outcome is also getting the thing that you wanted at the specification you wanted it in the time you wanted it (thing + specification + time = success). Processes also have performance indicators (though not all of them are *key* performance indicators) called enabling indicators to help predict if the goal will be achieved or not. What you measure in all of this is simply the number of successful process outcomes.

The Right Measure and the Right-Now Measure

Remember that everything is measurable. Literally everything—as long as your measurement includes the assumptions that allowed the measurement. I can measure the number of alien species that have visited Earth *if* I assume that all non-earthlings have checked in with me personally to be counted. Actually in this example, updated to match my assumptions, I'm not measuring the number of aliens who visit Earth; I'm measuring the number of aliens visiting Earth who check in with me (zero to date). Similarly, I can measure customer satisfaction if I assume that a positive response to a customer satisfaction survey is a measure of customer satisfaction. Of course, it's actually a measure of a survey respondent, who is a subset of all your customers. Hopefully a representative subset—but that's not guaranteed.

The point here is that very few measures are perfect (the number of fingers on your hand comes pretty close as long as you document whether a thumb is a finger), which means that most measures are flawed. Many people who want to measure something often believe that the choices are to know nothing (no measure) or know everything (perfect measure) and in the absence of everything will claim something isn't measurable. Those people miss out on actionable data. Flawed performance indicators are fine as long as you clearly state the flaws (in alien counting and customer satisfaction, for example).

In college, I took an art appreciation class. I was surprised to learn that it's not at all unusual for a painter to paint a picture, then come back and add more colors, more figures, more of everything, making it a different painting than the first one. The professor for this course said something that stuck with me: art is never "finished"—just "finished for now." Similarly, you may find yourself iterating on different measures until you get the one that best reflects the outcome of your process. Or your measure may get updated as you learn more about the data. It's more than OK to use what you have in order to take action while you iterate to get to something closer to perfect. If it helps you understand your business (or your customer, or your process) and it's actionable, it's useful.

Anecdote: New-Hire Training

I've worked in training for several years, and it's common for business leaders to want new-hire training to take less time. There is no escape from the cost of ramping up for new hires; it's either paid in wages or in training. Companies that pay higher wages for experienced employees can spend less time (money) training.

Employees either learn their jobs in training, from coworkers, or at the expense of customers. The challenge is to determine where to draw the lines between those sources of knowledge and experience.

Indicators in Tension

It's common, by the way, to have more than one success measure—even if they appear to be in conflict. Situations like that usually call for balancing metrics that may otherwise be in conflict. The classic example in project management is the three critical measures of time (delivering quickly), cost (delivering cheaply), and quality (delivering high quality), with the rule of thumb that you can have two of those but not all three. A project can be high quality and low cost, but it will take a long time. Another project can be fast and low cost, but quality will suffer. Or you can deliver high quality quickly, but it will be costly. While this may not be new information, what makes it relevant here is the need for balance. To balance the three legs of the stool that holds up project delivery, each leg has to have clearly defined terms. The law of diminishing returns states that there is a line after which more effort (higher quality, lower cost, faster delivery) doesn't deliver greater returns or greater satisfaction to the customer.

Building a KPI Map

I talked about the power of *how* as a way to clarify your mission and strategies. Now I'll show you how to keep track of all that at several levels of an organization. A KPI map is a diagram made up of mostly boxes and lines that illustrates the linear relationship between your mission and the strategies taken to achieve it.

When I begin work with a new consulting client, I start with a bunch of questions about their work, how they define success, and what they want to achieve. All that helps me understand their mission, strategies, and goals—the building blocks of their KPI map. I then always get a really big piece of paper and start connecting all those things into what eventually becomes a KPI map. The KPI map lets me (and more importantly, the client I'm working with) see the direct connection between their highest-level KPIs and their everyday tactics. And in between those tactics and the KPIs are all the strategies, goals, and processes that make it happen. In this chapter, we're going to build one of those KPI maps for Success Coffee.

Remember the peanut butter and jelly sandwich process that was made up of individual steps? Remember how each of those steps was also its own process with its own success measures? Your organization works the same way. Your mission is simultaneously what you want and the highest-level process in your organization. It is where all the efforts (all the processes) are aimed at the success of that mission (like a peanut butter and jelly sandwich). What don't always make it to the mission statement are the financial measures nestled directly beneath that mission. Because achieving a mission means you have to bring more money *in* than you pay *out*. A mission without financial measures is a just a pipe dream, while financial measures without a mission create a soulless organization that rarely lasts.

The KPI map itself is a living document that will evolve as your organization evolves or—more commonly —as your understanding of your organization evolves. But the process is easy, even if the results can be complicated. As we build the KPI map for Success Coffee, we will (of course) want to meet our mission and also make more money than we spend. Figuring that out just takes the power of how.

- *How will we make more money than we spend?*
- By increasing revenue and reducing the cost of our materials.
- *How will we reduce the cost of our materials?*
- By reducing the amount of milk wasted because of expiration.
- *How will we reduce the amount of expired milk?*

You see where this is going. Each of the answers to "how...?" becomes its own objective, which leads to a set of tactical steps, each of which has a measurable outcome. "How...?" is not an open-ended question; it's a specific question that needs a specific measurable answer.

Mission

The KPI map will look a bit like an organization chart, with your mission at the top underpinned by your financial measures, strategies (there will likely be more than one), goals (which are also process outcomes), and the tactics necessary (or at least planned) to improve. At each level is one or more objectives (make customers happy) as well as a measure (customer satisfaction percent). Essentially it's an expression that we want *this* to be true, and *this* is how we're measuring it. The KPI map will document the objectives and KPIs (and enabling indicators) at all levels of the organization.

That said, most organizations are too complex to capture every possible measure—particularly as your map gets more detailed. To understand this, think of the relationship between the mission and the KPIs like the relationship between a country and the individual streets in the country. It's definitely possible to create a country map with all the streets on it, but it's not always practical to try to look at all the levels at once.

Success Coffee Mission

Financial Measures

Right underneath your mission are boxes for revenue and cost because while all these strategies and goals are reflections of your mission, they're also either going to drive revenue *in* or drive cost *out*. Most of the financial measures under the mission on your KPI map will be some expression of revenue, cost, and profit. The money that comes into your organization will come from different sources, each of which will have a contribution to the overall revenue. The total revenue from all your sources will logically equal your total revenue. Similarly, costs break down into multiple categories (the largest of which is often payroll) that together make up the total cost picture.

If you're in the finance department or are in charge of a profit and loss statement (P&L) in your organization, you're likely to be the one determining which financial measures are the right ones. If you're anyone else in an organization, you may be reacting to those measures rather than defining them. That's not a reason to keep them off your KPI map, though—even if your team is all revenue or all cost. Keeping financial measures on your map ensures that you are keeping your eyes on that prize.

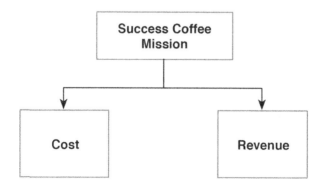

Strategy

Your strategy is *how* you'll impact the processes that support cost and revenue. Assume that you want to increase revenue (a pretty safe gamble). You'll ask the question, "How will we increase revenue?" To know that, you need to know what all the revenue sources are (at Success Coffee, all our revenue comes from either muffins or coffee). Once you know all those revenue sources—and more importantly, the relative contribution of each (e.g., one source that makes up 80 percent of revenue and seven other sources that together make up the remaining 20 percent)—how will you increase revenue? By (among other possibilities) increasing the number of Success Coffee customers and also increasing the average sales per customer.

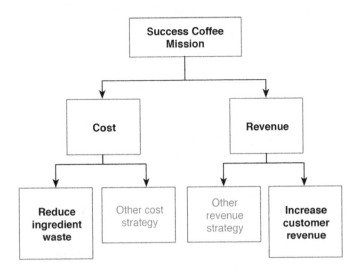

Goals

The question you asked for your strategy was "How will we increase customer revenue?" Including a goal makes that sentence more precise. "How will we increase customer revenue by X percent?" Your strategy is a statement of the processes you'll engage to achieve that mission, and goals are the outcomes of those processes. In most cases, the strategy and goal express a desired change within a single process that has a clear success measure. Goals are easily recognized by their verbs (increase, decrease, improve) since they are the actions taken in pursuit of a strategy.

Goals also usually apply to the outcome of a single process because if multiple processes are involved, there are likely multiple goals to pursue (at which point you're working on a strategy with multiple goals). Rather than focusing on hard-and-fast rules for what's a goal and what's not a goal, focus instead on how you'll take action. If there isn't a clear path of action, you may not have gotten specific enough in your goal. What makes a goal actionable? When you're reasonably assured that one intervention will impact all or most of the results within a category (or source). For Success Coffee, we'll increase customer revenue by increasing the average monthly customers from 1,441 to 1,585 and also by increasing the average sale per customer from $4.50 to $5.00. We'll also reduce our ingredient (in this case milk) waste by 16 percent (from thirty-one cartons per month to twenty-six cartons per month).

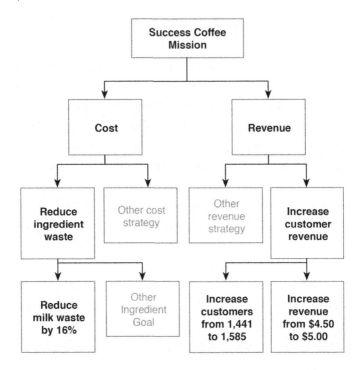

Tactics, Initiatives, and Projects

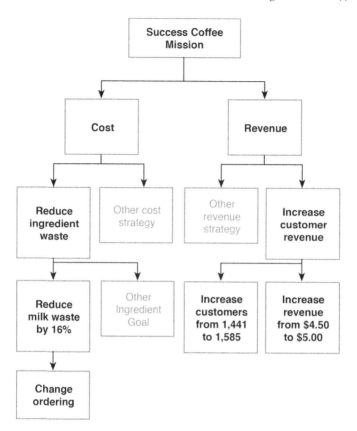

The day-to-day activity of measuring success usually involves milestones, dates, and owners. Tactics, initiatives, and projects are the specific and time-bound actions people take to improve process performance and meet goals. They often focus on the performance of humans or technology in order to produce more of something or to produce something at a higher quality. Tactics often get documented and tracked in project software with milestones, dates, deliverables, and owners. Within a given calendar year (or fiscal year, if that's different where you work), one goal can have several tactics, either worked on in sequence (one in each quarter, for example) or worked on in parallel (two different people working on two different tactics in support of one goal).

KPI Map for Success Coffee

Our mission at Success Coffee is to "build community by offering fresh-baked muffins and fresh-roasted espresso drinks in our neighborhood." Gross margin is our top-level financial KPI in support of that mission, and it's fed by total cost and total revenue. Of course, the problem with gross margin is that it's backward looking (as most KPIs are), which means that once we've missed our margin goal, it's too late to make it up. So we need to know the enabling indicators for gross margin that allow us to take action. In short, we need to build out this strategy.

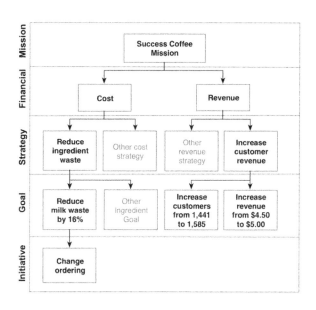

Success Coffee Strategies

We've priced our coffee with a modest margin and in line

with the competition. So how will we increase that margin? Either by reducing costs or increasing revenue. Let's start with revenue. There are a couple of paths to increased revenue:

1. More customers. This one is easy. If we have more people buying our coffee and muffins, we'll have more revenue. And if we serve more customers with the same indirect costs (e.g., during the same hours we're already staffing the coffee shop), we'll increase our margin.

One of the most costly activities in any organization is customer acquisition. In many cases, the entire marketing function is designed around getting more customers. This makes sense if you think about it. At Success Coffee, if we want new customers, we have to find ways to entice them away from their current favorite coffee shop or, even tougher, persuade them to start coming to a coffee shop when they don't usually do that. To increase the number of our customers, we need to know the baseline, or the current number, before we make any improvement.

2. Increased revenue per customer. This is a common measure in lots of industries because it's easier (which means cheaper) to influence the customers we already have to spend a little more than to acquire a brand-new customer. One path to increased revenue per customer is to increase prices, which many businesses do in response to inflation or increased materials cost (e.g., rising fuel costs increasing the price of delivery). For our purposes, we'll keep our prices the same, which means we'll generate more revenue per customer by selling more things to them.

Definition: Baseline

A baseline is a numeric representation of some KPI before action is taken to improve it. While it's not always possible to set a clear baseline in sales of a new product (that has so far had no sales because it's new), getting some kind of reference point allows you to know how much you improve (or fail to improve).

3. Use only fresh ingredients. Now let's talk about cost. One of our strategies is to reduce ingredient waste, which comes from our direct costs (along with indirect costs, one of our two cost categories at Success Coffee). Using fresh ingredients but controlling costs means controlling waste.

In many organizations (including our coffee shop) one of the biggest areas for reducing cost is to reduce waste or rework. The core of lean (a.k.a. lean manufacturing or lean production) is removing waste (there are seven different kinds!) from within processes. As I said, direct costs in our coffee shop include coffee beans, milk, flavoring syrup, muffins, cups, lids, and thermal sleeves. And the perishable ones are coffee beans, milk, and muffins, which become unsellable if we order too many, don't rotate our stock, or if sales fall. Our first direct cost goal then will be a reduction in food waste, which is to say money spent on food that doesn't make it to a paying customer.

In a larger organization, we might also have a goal around indirect costs, but since we're small, we'll stick with just a direct cost goal. That said, it's not uncommon for organizations of any size to bite off more than they can chew goal-wise. Knowing how much is a stretch and how much is enough is a moving target.

Success Coffee Goals

Remember that goals are process outcomes that are specific, measurable, achievable, results focused, and time bound. Goals are usually expressed for a single process change, and the actions taken to effect that process change are tactics, initiatives, or projects. As strategies are on executive dashboards and discussed by higher-ups, goal process outcomes have milestones and dates. Every process has a successful outcome, and goals are expressions of improvement in those successful outcomes (some improvement in "thing," "specification," or "time"). In practice, there will be more than one goal in pursuit of a strategy, just as there are multiple processes in support of a strategy. Process changes could include removing waste to improve productivity or otherwise making changes in the process steps to get to that outcome.

In all cases, goals are where action happens in making process-level changes. The tactics in pursuit of goals might result in updated training, buying new equipment, combining two departments' worth of work into one unified process to reduce handoff time, or any number of other process-level changes.

Increase the Number of Customers

Our strategic goal is to increase from 1,441 customers per month (the baseline) to 1,585 customers per month (the target). We first need to be sure we understand what's in that historic data. Is that 1,441 customers per month for last month only? Or is that an average over the past twelve months? If last month only, that's not enough history to understand the baseline. If that's twelve months, that's great! Anything in between (or greater than a year) will require some judgment about the value of that baseline.

Once you have a baseline, you'll likely want to know more about what's in it. Do all 1,441 customers come at the same time? The nature of our business may benefit from looking at customers per hour and customers per day to see what the patterns are. It's likely that we have more customers per hour in the early morning Monday through Friday and maybe more customers per hour in the midmorning on the weekends. Think back to the point that stuff is made up of other stuff and you'll see— if you haven't already—that monthly average customer counts are made up of daily average customer counts, which are made up of hourly average customer counts.

For Success Coffee, let's assume that our weekend

business is good, and we believe the best improvement opportunity is weekday business. The first part of setting our tactical goal is understanding that pattern. So one of us sits in the back of the coffee shop and counts the number of people who come in at each time. Or, if we're fancy, we look at the time stamp on each sales receipt. Either way, knowing the hourly volume gives us insight into whether we want to increase traffic during the already-busy times or if we want to increase traffic during the non-busy times.

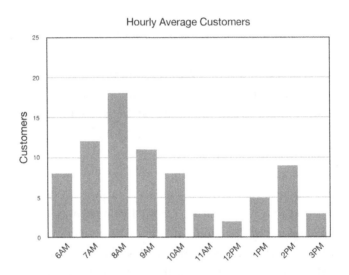

Increase the Revenue per Customer

Our strategic goal is to increase the average revenue per customer from \$4.50 to \$5.00. In our strategy, you saw that our revenue is made up of coffee drinks and muffins.

All the customers who come in buy a drink and half of the customers who come in buy a muffin. Our goal is to specifically make muffins attractive to the half of customers who don't buy one. Again, we've targeted a subset of the population rather than looking for a broad, sweeping solution.

Reduce Direct Costs

Our third strategic goal is to reduce direct costs. You'll remember that direct costs are those required to make our product (in this case a cup of coffee). Our direct costs are made up of espresso, milk, flavoring syrup, cups, lids, and sleeves. While increasing sales or customers will often come down to marketing or sales activity (like upselling), cost reduction is most often about reducing waste (or rework), the silent thief in most organizations. If your processes are heavily people dependent (instead of automated), have lots of handoffs between people or departments, or have lots of inputs and exits, you may have a lot of waste to eliminate. If waste is already mini-mal, cost reduction comes easiest with some significant process change, like automating some part of the process. In all cases, cost reduction, like customer increases and sales increases, starts with knowing where most of your costs are going.

At Success Coffee, 75 percent of the drinks we make have milk. The milk is poured into a pitcher and steamed, then added to the drink. We've observed that about 18 percent of the milk poured into the pitcher is not used in the drink and is wasted. An additional 16 percent of the milk we buy goes bad before we're able to use it. This expired milk (and the money we spent on it) goes directly down the drain. So our specific tactic to reduce cost associated with using fresh ingredients is to reduce milk waste.

Common KPIs

The United States Bureau of Labor Statistics classifies businesses as either goods producing (airplanes, apparel, and accordions) or services producing (banks, books, and baseball stadiums). Despite the incredibly wide range of goods and services offered by these organizations, their KPIs fall into a relatively small set of categories: financial, customer, employee, and productivity.

Financial KPIs

The two basic measures in any organization are revenue and cost. Revenue is definitely the sexiest of these—big sales get celebrated in ways that big savings rarely do. But don't discount the allure of a cost KPI. Having been on both the sales and the operations side, the lever on the revenue side is usually easier to see: sell more of a thing, or sell more of a more expensive thing, and sales increase. But there are usually more options for reducing cost, since there are usually more cost categories than revenue categories.

Revenue

I won't try to list all the different revenue types—that would take forever and wouldn't ever be complete. Basically this is money coming into the organization through sales, subscriptions, memberships, or some other channel.

Cost

- **Cost of goods sold (COGS)**—Also called direct costs, COGS include money spent to create the goods as well as the labor necessary to sell them.
- **Operating expenses (OPEX)**—Also called indirect costs, OPEX are everything necessary to run a business that's *not* directly related to creating and selling goods. These include things like rent, insurance, and office supplies.

Customer KPIs

If organizations were only run by metrics, customer service would be a defect (stay with me here). If we make a product or offer a service that's completely aligned to customer needs, and if our marketing and sales processes are on point, there is no need for customer service. And when there *is* a need for customer service, it's because something has gone wrong (defect). In practice, we know this isn't true. Good customer service can build loyalty and inspire repeat purchases.

Though revenue and cost are the highest KPIs—indicating an organization's ability to keep doing its thing—customer measures are often appropriately elevated to the same level as revenue and cost.

Common Customer KPIs

- **Customer satisfaction**—Many customer satisfaction measures are actually measures of *dis*satisfaction tracked by responses to questions on a survey. Surveys are usually cheap and quick, which is why they are so commonly used to get actionable data about satisfaction. Customer satisfaction can be measured for a specific transaction or as an overall perception.
- **NPS** (Net Promoter Score)—A kind of survey, NPS asks customers about their likelihood of recommending the product or services. Those scores are collated as either promoters, passives, or detractors. NPS is most useful as a perception survey (not a transaction survey) because it indicates perceived value and loyalty.
- **Customer engagement** (often a marketing measure)—This tracks customer activity like opening a marketing email or attending a webinar as a way of tracking engagement. The idea is that a higher engagement score is more likely to lead to a sale (or repeat sale).
- **Customer loyalty/retention**—Keeping

customers is usually cheaper than getting new ones. Customer retention, especially for subscription services (e.g., wireless telecommunications), measures efforts to keep customers happy and buying.

- **Repeat purchases**—More specific than loyalty, a customer who expresses loyalty is less valuable at the end of the day than one who makes a second (or third) purchase. However, dissatisfaction and repeat purchases can live together if customers perceive themselves as trapped into repeat purchases. These dissatisfied repeat buyers disappear at the first competitive opportunity.

- **Lifetime value**—Calculated to provide a long view of customer retention, lifetime value looks at how growing a relationship with an existing customer will have long-term benefits.

Employee KPIs

Employee KPIs shouldn't be confused with productivity KPIs, which are usually employees engaging in a process in pursuit of a successful outcome. The two are connected because productivity can positively impact retention, but for the purposes of measurement and improvement, they are separated here. So without productivity, employee KPIs are usually some version of retention or are subordinate to retention. Additionally, while compensation and benefits attract and keep talent and so are connected to employee KPIs, those are financial metrics.

Common Employee KPIs

- **Retention**—Once you spend the money and effort to recruit, hire, and train an employee, it's better to keep them than to start over with another one. For this reason, employee retention is a primary KPI, the inverse of which is attrition. Many organizations differentiate between regretted attrition (the ones you wish hadn't left) and unregretted attrition (the ones you fire). While the difference in designation between employees you ask to leave and those who leave on their own is important, both should be measured and improved. A robust practice of (for example) firing the lowest performers will highlight a failure in the recruiting or employee development programs rather than demonstrate high standards.
- **Engagement/Satisfaction**—If retention is the highest-level employee KPI, engagement and satisfaction are enabling indicators because low engagement is absolutely a predictor of regretted attrition.
- **Internal mobility**—Another predictor of regretted attrition is lack of internal mobility. Employees who have a chance to increase their pay by doing something new or

something with more responsibility are usually more likely to remain with the company.

Productivity

Productivity refers to the percentage of available resources (usually time or money) that actually create customer or sellable value. Productivity is usually an expression of successful process outcomes, while defects and waste are the inverse expression (attempts – successes = waste). Rework is usually an outcome of a productivity miss and is included in productivity KPIs. I won't try to list all the possible process defects for all the possible industries here. While they have differences and nuances, they all roll back to productivity.

Common Productivity KPIs

- **Utilization** (employees or machines)—This is essentially the percentage of time someone is available for work during which they actually do productive work.
- **Throughput**—Usually expressed as a rate, this is the number of units able to move completely through a process within a given period of time: calls answered per hour, Pop-Tarts baked per minute, or airplanes painted per week.
- **Time to competency**—This is often a training measure, particularly for new hires. The time

between someone's first day and when they're fully productive is not wasted time, but organizations want to be sure that time is always optimized. The corporate training industry works hard on techniques to bridge that gap.

6

HOW TO MEASURE

I have been struck again and again by how important measurement is to improving the human condition.

— Bill Gates

Everything is measurable. The degree of precision may vary from one measure to the next, but in my experience, so far it's always been possible to inform a decision with at least some data. And if I haven't mentioned it already, despite attempts by many super-smart folks to make it more complicated, measurement is just counting, and we all learned to do that a long time ago. The finance wonks, business intelligence pros, and various other math nerds are winding up their protests, and of course they're right: the more complex the organization or problem, the more complex the measurement. But I say always start easy; there's plenty of time to get complicated later. For our purposes, KPIs are just counting. Frequency of occurrence, the amount of money, the length of time, the size, the weight—all of these are countable.

The trick is simply documenting your assumptions. If I want to measure safety, I might assume that lost-time injuries are the right measure of a lack of safety (hence "days without an injury" posters in some manufacturing and construction workplaces). If I want to track purchases made by repeat customers, I might measure sales of accessories with the assumption that accessory purchasers already purchased the related product (therefore are repeat customers). If I'm measuring the temperature in my house, I'm assuming that the thermometer in the hallway represents the temperature in every part of the house (it doesn't).

This is also a useful trick for estimating the effort it will take to do something. I might, for example, assume that I can perform brain surgery in four hours, which includes the assumption that I'm a brain surgeon (I'm not, so the flawed assumption means this measure will fail). We make assumptions like these all the time and usually don't even think about them, which ends up being a consistent source of miscommunication. But really, it's easy. If I measure my wealth by the number of nickels in my right front pocket, I'm assuming that (1) all my nickels are in my right front pocket, (2) coins of other denominations don't count, and (3) I have no other sources of wealth.

What the Data Says and What the Data Means

Documenting assumptions helps you remember that the thing you're trying to understand and the thing you're measuring aren't the same. Ideally your data will lead you directly to draw obvious conclusions and take action, but it's not a guarantee. Sales seems like a pretty straight-forward example. Strong sales of a new product to existing customers may mean they needed it all along, or it may mean that your marketing was compelling.

Think of a map of the neighborhood where you live. The map may call out the street names and main land-marks, but there isn't any way a single map can describe everything about a neighborhood. In fact, cartography (the science of mapmaking) can show way more inter-esting maps of neighborhoods, including a streetlight map, a weather map, a grocery store map, or a density map. Each of these is one aspect—one measure—of the neighborhood, but none is the same as the neighborhood itself. Similarly, your KPI is an indicator—not the real thing—and will show you one view.

Data Rich and Action Poor

Most organizations I've worked with are data rich and action poor, meaning they spend most of their available time sorting through and making meaning of an ocean of data and little time improving their processes (and outcomes).

Like Goldilocks and her experience with some bears, you will likely find yourself either with too much, too little, or just enough data for what you need to act on. In today's world, the most common problem by far is wading through the ocean of available data to get to the data that you need. In preparation for this book, I thought this would be the place I would include some staggering statistics about the amount of data available in the world. But each reference I read had bigger and bigger numbers based on what year the study was done. By one estimate, 2.5 billion gigabytes (GB) of data was generated every day in 2012, and as of this writing, that was several years ago—years during which data production hasn't slowed down. My point is that if you haven't yet come across a situation where you have too much data rather than not enough, you will.

There are definitely also situations where you want to know something, and there isn't any data—or any accessible data. If you're lucky, you'll get to have a conversation with someone who knows the data is "in there somewhere" and can help find it. If you're less lucky, you'll find yourself collecting your own data. Data collection tools can be as simple as manual observations checked on a sheet of paper or a survey. These are not as deep and detailed as automated data collected in a spreadsheet, but they are still better than nothing at helping you make decisions.

Data Types

You don't have to become an expert in all data types and collection methods to measure success. It *is* important that you become familiar enough to understand the flaws in a measure (they all have flaws) and to have easier conversations with the data professionals.

For most organizational measurement activities, data will fall into two categories: qualitative (like focus groups) and quantitative (numbers). Both are necessary, though usually only quantitative data gets elevated to KPI status.

That said, the best display of KPI progress includes a combination of both. Qualitative data are sometimes called testimonials or anecdotes. One customer's anecdote can provide critical nuance to an otherwise dry quantitative presentation.

Tip!
Don't get wrapped around the axle with all these data descriptions. Because your KPIs are a count of successful process outcomes, and those outcomes are a combination of discrete and continuous data (thing + spec + time), your KPIs are probably nominal data (mine are). The tactical and strategic measures that support KPIs are often made up of different data types.

What data you measure matters because measuring the wrong thing will either mask defects or will prevent you from seeing improvement you're making. This is mostly because what you measure should be the most accurate possible reflection of the goal you're seeking. For example, if you have a goal related to customer satisfaction, and your data set is the number of defects in customer orders, you're missing an important measure (because defects in orders isn't a measure of satisfaction—it's a measure of defects in orders).

Quantitative and **qualitative** data often get compared to each other to determine which is better, but it's more useful to see them as complementary. They are two great things that go great together. How often have you gotten a set of data values and wanted to know more about the story behind a data point? "I know that this survey respondent said they are dissatisfied, but I don't know why." These two data collection methods should feed into each other to create a better picture overall. When a complex data set leaves you wondering why, schedule a focus group or series of interviews. When your focus group or interviews are leaving you wondering how wide-spread those opinions are, send out a survey. Or even better, look for evidence of behavior matching those opinions in your data. If focus group opinions are that technology early adopters are fine with a bug-ridden beta product as a trade-off for new tech, find out how many of your beta product purchasers or testers are early adopters.

~

Anecdote: Vital Signs

Imagine checking someone's vital signs every day for a year and tabulating that data (quantitative) or spending thirty minutes on the first day of every month during that same year asking about someone's day (qualitative).

The 365 data points would show patterns in vital signs on days of the week or by season. The thirty-minute conversations would yield a depth of information not captured in the vitals data. Trying to determine which of these is better misses the coolness of finding meaning in both approaches to information collection and categorization.

Qualitative data is more nuanced and is generally less countable than quantitative. Think of a three-hour focus group with five people giving you feedback on a new program you want to launch. You'll hear lots of detailed information and feedback, but the value will be in the nuance of the conversation and not in counting the number of times someone said a specific word. Qualitative data can get a bad rap because there usually isn't as much of it as quantitative data, and it's sometimes considered "soft" data. But that three-hour focus group may introduce ideas or nuanced feedback that terabytes of "hard" data would never have captured. The most common qualitative data that makes it to a KPI list is taking verbatim customer feedback (often something they type into an open text field in a survey) and making it quantitative by counting the number of positive versus negative responses. Other than that or something similar, KPIs should be quantitative data.

Qualitative Data Types and Collection

- **Interviews**—Interviews are an opportunity to ask, among other questions, "What should I ask you that I haven't asked yet?" Although you come to an interview probably wanting some specific information, there is an opportunity to learn things you didn't even know you wanted to know—something that will potentially inform later collection of quantitative data. Prepare for your interview by having a small set of questions you *must* ask followed by questions you'd like to ask if you have time. Leave plenty of time for conversation, and let the interviewees' answers guide you at least as much as your own questions. Because if all you wanted was clear concise answers, you could have sent an email questionnaire.

- **Focus groups**—Sometimes you don't even know the questions to ask, and for those times, focus groups are your friend. Be very specific about whom you choose for your focus group. There are plenty of professional research firms who will prescreen focus group attendees to be sure that you get the best information. Focus groups of fewer than five people or more than ten people are less effective than those between five and ten. Your expectation is not just for the focus group attendees to respond to your questions but also for them to interact and respond to each other. This additional interaction is where some of the richest data can come. Prepare to have someone record (video and audio) the entire thing so you can squeeze every drop of information out of the experience.

- **Surveys**—Surveys are underrated in my experience. Criticism of survey data is often that because surveys are people reporting about themselves (self-reported data), and because people are rarely completely objective about themselves, the data is flawed. While this is true to some degree, individual biases in survey data are often washed out in a large enough sample. Similarly, there can be a known bias (I've often found that salespeople uniformly estimate greater month-end sales results at the beginning of the month than usually materialize at the end of the month). In situations where the flaw is evenly spread across the whole population, good survey-question writing or judicious analysis can prevent that bias from negatively impacting the decisions made. On the plus side, surveys are usually fast, cheap ways to get large amounts of data. I use surveys consistently— even for initial or directional data to inform next steps.

Quantitative data is countable, like the number of coffee beans in a pound, the number of minutes a customer waits on hold, or the number of cups of coffee sold at Success Coffee. In order for quantitative data to be most useful, you'll need a lot of it spread out over time. More on that in the section about statistics. (Don't fear them—statistics are your friend.)

Quantitative Data Types

There are different types of quantitative data, which is mostly important for knowing the best ways to analyze and visualize it. Data is either categorical or numerical, and both types (and their subordinate types) are useful in establishing KPIs.

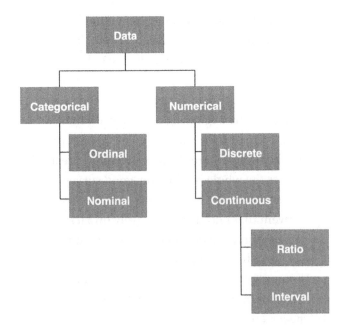

A. **Categorical** data is what it sounds like: categories. Those categories can be either ordinal, where the order of the categories matters, or nominal, where the order doesn't matter.

A1. **Nominal data**—The word "nominal" has the same origin as the word "name," which makes it easy to remember. Success Coffee sells blueberry muffins and banana nut muffins. If we count the number of blueberry muffins and the number of banana nut muffins in a pastry display, we have put muffins into categories by nominal data. The individual categories aren't different from each other in any way that is described by the name (or category), nor does it matter how we order that data. A bar chart of all the muffins by flavor can be in any order (though the general standard is that the category with the most occurrences would be on the left).

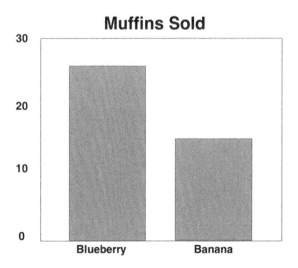

A2. Ordinal data—Ordinal data is also categorical, but the order matters. It's similarly easy to remember because "ordinal" and "order" have the same origin. Customer satisfaction is often measured on an ordinal scale:

- How satisfied are you with your muffin choice?
- Extremely dissatisfied
- Dissatisfied
- Neutral
- Satisfied
- Extremely satisfied

In ordinal data the specific value of each category or the measurable value *between* categories isn't known, but the order matters. A bar chart of satisfaction responses should be presented in order rather than choosing (for example) to put the most frequently occurring value (in this case, "satisfied") at the far left.

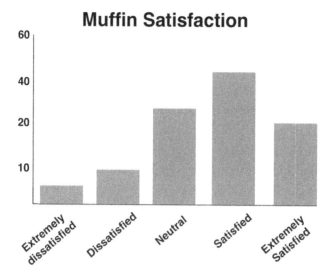

B. **Numerical data** is made of numbers and is either discrete or continuous. Purists will say that discrete data can be counted but not measured and that continuous data can be measured but not counted. This is technically true, but for the purposes of measuring KPIs, it isn't relevant. KPIs are successful process outcomes which can be discrete, continuous, or a combination. Similarly, process outcomes that fail to meet the specification (defects) are also countable. In both cases, even though those outcomes will include both discrete and continuous data types (thing + spec + time), they are countable.

B1. **Discrete data** is numerical data that counts whole things that can't be broken into smaller things. The number of cars that come off an assembly line, the number of stars within a hundred light years of Earth, or the number of bars in your neighborhood are all discrete data. That's because cars, stars, and bars can't be broken down into smaller versions of themselves. There are no half bars and no partial cars. A car can be broken into its parts, but then you're measuring parts, not cars. So a count of steering wheels is also a count of discrete data.

B2. **Continuous data** can be continuously broken into smaller bits without changing the nature of the measure. Years can be months, weeks, days, hours, or minutes, and the data retains its structure. Continuous data has further categories and can either be continuous interval data or continuous ratio data.

B2a. **Continuous interval data** refers to ordered units that have the same difference between the values but for which zero doesn't mean "nothing" (for which there is no absolute zero). A classic example of interval data is temperature. The difference between twenty degrees and thirty degrees is the same as the difference between thirty degrees and forty degrees. However, while there is zero degrees, that value is not the *absence* of temperature.

B2b. **Continuous ratio data** also refers to ordered units that have the same difference between the values, but in ratio data, zero indicates "nothing." A classic example of ratio data is weight, because the difference between two grams and three grams is the same difference as that between three grams and four grams, *and* because a weight measure of zero is possible.

Quantitative Data Collection

Direct observation—Direct observation can seem like qualitative data collection, but you're not asking the open-ended questions you would in a qualitative study. Instead, you're observing and tracking specific behaviors or transactions. Direct observation is more time consuming than if you have the data in a database, but don't dismiss it as a method. Often you can get quick direct observation data that provides plenty of information to take you to the next step. Some methods of direct observation include the following:

Transaction analysis—In a situation where a transaction (a customer email, a lost sale, an injury report) is well documented, you can conduct a detailed analysis of those transactions for specific patterns or repeated behaviors. Technically this isn't direct observation because you're collecting data after the transaction has happened, but decent record keeping means there is much to learn right at your fingertips.

Assessments and tests—Tests are a great way to collect information and data about knowledge or skill level and to simultaneously reinforce that knowledge or skill. In some ways, tests provide more reliable information than surveys because they require knowledgeable responses, not just opinions. Most of the comments here about assessments and tests apply to humans. Testing machines or technology is a whole different process, and data collected that way is more consistently predictive of the behavior of machines or technology.

Databases—Databases are their own awesome quantitative data collection method. A database is an organized collection of individual data points that can be filtered and searched (queried) for specific subsets of the data. There are tons of books written and careers made on the creation and management of databases, which I won't try to replicate here. In the explosion of data we live in these days, you can rightly assume that there is more data sitting in a database than you are aware of. (In fact, it's probably not good to think about that too much.) It is not my intent here to teach you how to build or use databases but instead to help you have a useful conversation with a database professional or business analyst.

If you've ever used (or even looked at) a Microsoft Excel spreadsheet, you already have an idea of basic database elements. Similarly, if you have a smartphone, your contacts list is a database that will help illustrate these common terms. The data in a database is about one or more subjects (sometimes called objects) that could be friends (in the case of your smartphone contact list), customers, employees, sales, office buildings, or some other identifiable subject.

Definition: Data

The term "data" is technically the plural of the word "datum," though in practice "data" is usually used for both.

Data point—The smallest unit of information in a database is an individual point of data about a subject. In Microsoft Excel, this is contained in the intersection of a row and a column, called a cell. In your smartphone contacts list, an example could be Springfield, the city where your friend José (one of your contacts) lives.

Field (or column or attribute)—A database needs to have at least one field to contain the attributes of your subjects. In Excel this is an individual column that in your smartphone contacts might be labeled as "city" and would contain the city for each record in your database.

Record (or row)—Each individual subject in a database gets its own row, which makes it an individual record. In your smartphone, José would be one record that includes several fields likely including his last name, the city he lives in (Springfield), his email address, and his phone number.

Table (or file)—A table is a collection of attributes (columns) for individual subjects (records). All the contacts in your smartphone make up a table. Tables can have hundreds of fields (columns) and hundreds of thousands of records or can have only a few of each.

Database—A collection of tables makes up a database. You might have tables for your customers, your sales, and your employees. All of these make up your database.

Relational database—This is a collection of tables linked by common fields. Relational databases are super-cool and allow the comparison of data within tables. You could find customers (from the customer table) who had bought a specific product (sales table) from a specific salesperson (employee table).

Metadata—While not a separate part of a database, metadata is an important term in understanding data. Think of metadata as data *about* data. Examples could be the data author, the file size, or the time and date of the creation of the data. It's less important that you know the precise definition of metadata in all circumstances and more important that you know how the term is used in *your* organization's data structure.

Getting data out of a database consists of knowing enough SQL (which is pronounced "sequel" and stands for Structured Query Language, but no one says that) to run your own query or knowing someone who can help you get the data. The more familiar you are with these database terms, the easier it will be to run your own query or get someone who can.

Trusting Your Data

Before you get all giddy about how much data you have to tell your KPI story, you'll want to be able to trust your data. There are two important checks of data collection methodologies to determine whether they are reliable and whether they're valid. Checks of validity and reliability have the greatest rigor in a written assessment where you can conduct statistical analysis of patterns of responses for these tests. In nonassessment situations, the validations can be less rigorous but are no less important.

Reliability means that your method measures the same things in the same ways over and over. A personality test taken by the same person several times with several different results is an unreliable instrument. In database queries, there are ways to spot-check the data to be sure that everything in it is supposed to be in it (and everything *not* in it is supposed to not be in it).

Validity is the degree to which your measurement instrument measures what it's supposed to measure. One popular example is the ongoing argument about the SAT (Scholastic Aptitude Test), which is used by many colleges to predict the likelihood of college success. Some studies have named the SAT invalid, claiming that it doesn't predict college success as much as it predicts test-taking success. In practice, validity can simply be a gut check that the data point you're looking at represents what you think it does in the real world.

Definition: Litmus Test

In the fourteenth century, scientists discovered that a mixture of organic compounds would change color in the presence of an acidic or alkaline solution. Since then, the term "litmus test" is often used to describe a way to validate a wide variety of measures.

KPI Litmus Test

If I can pull a ridiculous lever and achieve the objective, it's not a good KPI. Need to increase gross sales? Triple the marketing budget (or hire twice as many salespeople). Need to cut costs? Get rid of half your staff. In both these examples, the simple answer is easy if you ignore the health of the business and the other KPIs. Whenever it's possible to create dramatic change in one KPI by pulling a single lever, always look to see if another KPI is victimized as a result. The classic balance between cost, quality, and time is an important verification. If you decide to go much faster in a process, it's likely that cost or quality will be impacted.

Success Coffee Data

At Success Coffee, our strategic goal is to reduce direct cost (the cost of wasted milk) while (of course) increasing revenue per customer and increasing the number of customers. Using our KPI litmus test, the easiest way to reduce the costs of goods sold is to buy less of them from our suppliers! Of course, that means we have less to sell, so that's no good as a strategy.

Data at Success Coffee comes from a combination of quantitative and qualitative sources. Our point-of-sale system tracks all our sales transactions. From that database, we can get overall revenue, revenue per transaction, revenue per day, and tons of other splits of the data. We also have a simple accounting system that gives us data on indirect costs (like utilities) and direct costs (like milk). We have manual data collection for expired milk: each time someone throws away an unopened gallon of milk because it's expired, they put a check mark on the sheet of paper by the carton recycle bin. We also review comments on social media (e.g., Yelp) for qualitative data.

We've established already that a KPI is the process outcome (thing) + the specification + the time it took to deliver it. The success measure is the frequency that all three conditions are met.

Thing—This is simply the number of times that the process outcome is completed minus any work in progress (incompletes) that is still within the time expectation. For a transaction process, this is the number of completed transactions. For a manufacturing process, it's the number of completely manufactured widgets (or ball bearings or airplanes). The count of completed "things" should include failed specs and failed timings because those failures are important defect measures (e.g., incomplete outcomes as a percent of attempts). The challenge here is to decide specifically what defines "complete." Because processes connect to other processes and are subsets of processes (stuff is made up of other stuff), the line for where a process ends is sometimes a judgment decision.

Specification—Most organizations define "quality" as the degree to which a product or service meets the specification. In manufacturing, this is usually the physical characteristics including weight, thickness, diameter, or some other physical measure of what the customer needs for the product. In a service organization, the spec is also measured by what the customer needs (or wants) and is usually defined by measures of satisfaction (or dissatisfaction). The count is the number of complete outcomes that meet the specification. The "thing" count minus the ones that fail the specification is the count of quality defects.

Time—Whether measured in months, weeks, days, or fractions of seconds, there is a target time for how long it takes to produce a thing at the specification. Counting (1) the outcomes that (2) met the spec (3) within the specified time is the measure of success.

Definition: Rate vs. Frequency

The terms rate and frequency overlap in their definitions. Frequency is the number of occurrences (e.g., phone calls) per unit of time (e.g., per hour). Rate can be the number of occurrences per unit of time and can also be the number of occurrences (e.g., sales) per other non-time occurrence (e.g., salesperson).

Context Matters

Process outcomes that fail the quality spec, fail the time spec, or simply fail to complete are defects for that process. While you should definitely measure each of those things, the high-level measure is the number of successes divided by the number of attempts, which gets to the success *rate* (the inverse of which is the defect rate). That is to say, successes as a stand-alone measure don't provide needed context.

We might say sales was $72,000, that we have 843 satisfied customers, or that there were 16 failed transactions. In each of these, the metric is only interesting for a moment before you end up with more questions (which is appropriate).

Providing the context makes these much more descriptive: $72,000 in sales with an average unit price of $1.03 is a better description. As is 843 satisfied customers out of 7,000 customers and 16 failed transactions out of 10,000 attempted transactions. In each case, the better measure is the *rate* of something within the context of a broader list of possible options, and this is usually expressed as a percentage.

Each of these examples (and a zillion more) provides

more precise and useful information than the original measure itself. Traveling sixty miles is interesting but out of context doesn't say much. Traveling sixty miles *per hour* or sixty miles *per day* says way more, and that added context gives us more to work with.

~

Tip!
Statistics are just a tool. Their entire job is to help you understand and make decisions about a lot of things (or people) while only having access to a few things (or people).

Statistics Are Your Friend

Somewhere there is a statistic about a fear of statistics, but ironically, the people who suffer from that particular phobia wouldn't ever know that statistic. I was not a student in school who loved math, and I did what I could to skate by. In the community college I attended soon after high school, I took a course called Business Statistics. Whether because of my math aversion or the full-time job I worked before going to classes at night, I loathed this class. To this day, it remains the largest gap on my "permanent record" because when I realized that in preparation for the midterm exam, I had done exactly none of the homework, I simply didn't go back. Ironically enough, the math I most often use today for my work is statistics.

Statistics is simply a series of mathematical methods of collecting, analyzing, and presenting data for purposes of understanding a population. Population in this case is the entire group of people, places, or things about which you want to collect, analyze, or present data. Statistics come in two types: descriptive and inferential.

Descriptive statistics, as the term implies, are used to describe a set of data (and what the data stands for). If you have tested tensile strength (how far you can stretch something before it breaks) for one bag of licorice, you could use descriptive statistics to describe the results of those tests. If there are fifty pieces of licorice in the bag, your statistics would express data collected during your tensile strength tests (like the average pounds of tension applied before the licorice broke) although then you would have fifty pieces of broken licorice.

Inferential statistics would allow you to determine the likelihood that the results of your tests on that one bag were predictive of all bags of licorice (maybe from that store or from that supplier). This is because inferential statistics allow statements about a population based on the results of a sample. One of the best-known uses of both descriptive and inferential statistics is in the census. It's not possible to literally count every human in the United States (or most other countries), so the United

States Census Bureau takes a sample of the population and draws conclusions about the whole United States based on that relatively small population. They use descriptive statistics to describe the responses of the people in the sample and inferential statistics to infer things about the population (including people who were not surveyed).

~

Anecdote: Ancient Statistics

One of the earliest known uses of statistics was recounted (pun intended) by ancient historian Thucydides in his *History of the Peloponnesian War*. Apparently Athenian soldiers counted the number of bricks in a nearby section of wall in order to estimate the height of ladders needed to scale the walls. The war didn't work out so well for Athens in the end but not for lack of clever statistical techniques.

Rolling the Dice

Statistics began from probability, which is the science of likelihood. Probability tries to create order out of a chaotic universe (who doesn't love that?) by predicting the likelihood of a future occurrence (an outcome) based on present conditions. When calculated, probability is a value between zero (no chance of the thing happening) and one (the thing will definitely happen).

In classic probability, often illustrated with coin flipping and die tossing, the total number of possible outcomes is known. A coin toss has two possible outcomes: heads or tails—if we assume an edge landing is not possible (remember assumptions?). A coin tossed will land and display either heads or tails. If my desired outcome is heads, that's one out of two possible outcomes, so the probability of getting heads on a toss is one divided by two or .5 (halfway between zero and one). That doesn't mean you won't toss two times and get two heads in a row. Remember that probability is the science of *likelihood*, not *certainty*. So as you toss that coin more and more, your results will trend toward that 50 percent, but—especially in fewer tosses—the numbers may not match exactly.

Statistical Significance

In analyzing your data, you will likely get to decide (or you'll be asked) whether your data conclusions are statistically significant. If you're not familiar with the idea of statistical significance, here it is in a nutshell: results are significant if they are mathematically likely to be due to a specific cause rather than randomly or by chance.

In many cases, applying statistical significance is overkill, but there are some situations where that's not true.

1. If making hiring, firing, promotion or other HR decisions
2. If the money saved or spent will show up on some important person's monthly or quarterly report
3. If you have an important point to make (in which case it will be even easier to make it if your results are statistically significant)

~

Tip!
Unlike in scientific experimentation, collecting enough data to establish statistical significance often isn't necessary (or practical) in business settings.

Some Easy Statistical Tools

Sampling—When you don't have a chance to study every item or person in a population (e.g., the census), using statistical sampling can help you draw reliable conclusions about a population based on a sample. Keep in mind that in statistics, "random sample" means something very specific, and if you use that term without a specific methodology, expect to get questions.

There are two variables you get to plan. First is confidence level: literally your mathematical confidence that the results of the sample match the results of the population. A confidence level of 95 percent is usually acceptable in a business setting. The other variable is the confidence interval, also called the margin of error. When a value is reported as "twenty-four with a confidence interval of five," that means the value could be up to five points above or below (so a range of nineteen to twenty-nine).

Correlation—In the absence of a direct causal relationship (clear evidence that one thing caused another), correlation data is useful insight. Correlation measures the degree to which two data sets *change* like each other. A classic example is ice cream sales (in dollars) and ambient temperature (in degrees Fahrenheit). Very often a rise in ambient temperature will happen at the same time as a rise in ice cream sales. While it's wrong to infer that the temperature *caused* the increase in ice cream sales (or even more diabolical, the opposite), it is informative to know that these data sets trend together. If nothing else, the ice cream shop owner can predict a similar sales increase next summer. That's called a positive correlation: the values go up together.

A negative correlation is two data sets that trend opposite each other. Keeping with the ambient temperature example, there is a strong negative correlation between the ambient temperature and layers of clothing worn by people outside. The higher the temperature, the fewer layers. Correlation is always between negative one and positive one, and the closer to one of those numbers, the stronger the correlation. A correlation score of zero indicates no relationship between the two data sets. Microsoft Excel makes correlation really easy.

Measures of central tendency—Classic measures of descriptive statistics are the mean, median, and mode (measures of central tendency). These are easy ways to describe a data set, the most common of which is the mean, which is the same as the average. An average is great because it's one number that describes a whole data set. The problem with an average value is that it smooths out what could be a wide range of values, so it's always useful

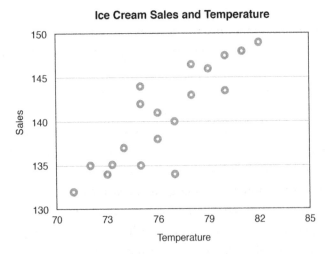

Ice Cream Sales and Temperature

to look at what the central measures may be masking. The median is the value that, when data is numerically ordered, has the same frequency of data points before it and after it. The mode is the value that occurs most frequently. As a rule of thumb, measures of central tendency each have their own limitations, so you should be careful about drawing conclusions with only one of those values.

Normal distribution—Probability theory, upon which statistics is founded, states that most data sets will fall into a predictable overall pattern, and it's surprising how often this ends up being true. In most data sets, more data points will cluster close to mean (the average), and fewer data points will be farther from the mean. The visual effect is a line chart often described as a bell curve.

How you display your data matters. There are some people who can look at a data table and understand the trends, the highs and lows, the problems, and the wins. For the rest of us, we need charts and graphs. Data visualization is part science, part art, and part marketing. There are stories to tell in any data set that will be defined by how you display it; more importantly your audience's ability to understand the story will depend on how well you display it. The visualization choices you make (which kind of charts, the scale, what gets highlighted, what gets excluded) can guide your audience to the conclusions you want.

The key point to data visualization is that it's just communication. And like any communication, it can be simple and elegant, dense and complicated, or even misleading. How you display your data matters. Here are some data visualization points.

Likert scales—Surveys often ask for responses on a one-to-five (or ten, or whatever) scale where one is bad and five is good (often called a Likert scale). On a survey of Success Coffee customers, an average score of 4.0 (out of a possible 5.0) for a thousand survey responses seems great, but that average might hide a small but critical set of ones and twos behind a bunch of fives. So there's a better way to tell that story. Displaying Likert scale data in three categories: positives (fours and fives), neutrals (threes) and negatives (ones and twos) provides a more actionable view. By seeing the count (or percentage) of negative responses separate from neutral and positive responses, it's easier to identify improvements than if the scores are all lumped together in an average. This is sometimes called "top-two, bottom-two," or for a ten-point Likert scale for Net Promoter Score (NPS), promoters (nine to ten), passives (seven to eight), and detractors (one to six).

Chart scale—The x-axis on a chart is the horizontal bottom axis, and the y-axis is the vertical side, and it's easiest for me to remember x from y by visualizing the vertical line that makes up the bottom of the y. Building a chart requires you to pick a scale (the interval between the points on your axis), although many software programs will automatically choose the scale if you let them. If the scale you choose for a line or bar chart is too small, small differences in your data look huge, and conversely, too large a scale hides important differences. Choose a scale that shows the variability in your data. Most importantly, if you report on the same data more than once (weekly or monthly, for example), be sure to use the same scale from report to report so you don't end up hiding or falsely inflating trends.

Line charts—Line charts are great for seeing trends

over time, particularly because a line chart will show the trend *between* time intervals. If the number of wasted gallons of milk at Success Coffee goes from ten at the end of week one to fifteen at the end of week two, it's likely that the number was somewhere around thirteen on Wednesday of week two. The line between those two points will slope upward to fifteen, showing not just the week-over-week change but the buildup as well.

That said, choosing your time period is critical for the story you're telling. The week-over-week story may hide that the increase in wasted milk happened entirely on the last day of the week, which is a very different story than an evenly distributed increase. Line charts also make it easy to visualize multiple data sets on the same chart, but it doesn't take many different lines for a line chart to get so busy that it's unreadable. Again, think of the story you're telling and what best brings that story forward.

Scatter plot (*x-y* graph)—Scatter plots (or scatter diagrams) are used to display correlation (one of my favorite data displays). Correlation, you'll recall, is the relationship between two variables. Specifically, it measures the degree to which the variables *change* together. Calculating correlation returns a single numeric value ranging between negative one and positive one that expresses that relationship. The scatter plot illustrates that relationship over time and across a set of data points rather than as a single number. A correlation coefficient of one is a perfect positive relationship and on a scatter plot looks like a perfectly balanced upward sloping line. But that's boring (and rarely exists in the wild), and so the scatter plot will visually show either a widely "scattered" data set where there is low correlation or a tightly "scattered" data set with high correlation, including outliers (which always have their own interesting story to tell). In the below scatter plot, the correlation coefficient is .7422, which is a moderately strong positive correlation. While the number is accurate, the scatter plot shows the variation in the data points.

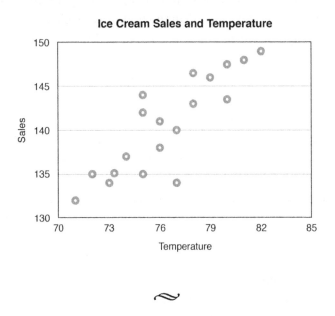

Ice Cream Sales and Temperature

~

Bar charts (or column charts)—Bar charts can be either vertical (sometimes also called column charts) or horizontal and are great for comparing data in discrete categories like quarterly sales, types of workplace injuries, or categories of waste. They are most effective when the categories have clear boundaries (a sale can't be in both Q1 and Q2). Bar charts can easily show up to four variables: proportionate contribution (in a stacked bar), frequency of occurrences, percent contribution (on the y-axis), and categories (on the x-axis).

Definition: Pareto Charts

Pareto charts and Pareto analysis are named for Vilfredo Pareto. He was an Italian scientist who found (among a lot of other things) that 80 percent of the land in Italy in the early twentieth century was owned by 20 percent of the population. This led to the 80/20 rule, which is named after him.

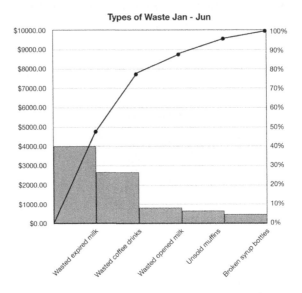

Pareto chart—This is a blend of a column and line chart with the intent of displaying the Pareto principle (that 80 percent of effects come from 20 percent of causes). In creating a Pareto chart, the y-axis represents frequency of occurrences, and the x-axis represents categories. The category with the highest frequency is placed to the far left, the category with the second-highest frequency is placed next to that, and so on, resulting in an ordered set of bars. Then a line chart measuring cumulative percent contribution is laid over the bar chart so that the line starts at zero and is drawn to the top-right corner of the far-left bar (this is easier to see visually). The next point on the line is the percent contribution of the first bar *and* the second bar, the third point is the percent contribution of the first three bars, and so on. The effect, assuming an 80/20 balance, is that your audience can see which categories make up about 80 percent of the effect. Below is a Pareto chart of the top kinds of waste at Success Coffee from January to June.

Pie charts—I'll admit it, I'm not a fan of pie charts. They are effective for showing proportions of a whole but not much else. Pie charts always measure percentages of the whole but can show an additional value by putting the number in the text field rather than the percentage (which is then estimated from the pie slice). But even then, it's one exact value and one inferred from relative slices. An expanded pie chart can drill down two levels, which can be a useful visualization. An expanded pie chart pulls one slice out from the rest of the pie and shows a further breakdown of what's in that slice.

Comparing Different Data

Getting to a common denominator is necessary to be able to compare things that are not alike (like apples and oranges). You remember from math class how to add fractions together. If you need to add one-half and two-thirds together, you have to first establish a common denominator. There are several for this fraction, but multiplying the two denominators together to get 6 (2 x 3 = 6) is the easiest way. 1/2 = 3/6, and 2/3 = 4/6. Now we can add them together and get 7/6, or 1 and 1/6. While technically associated with adding fractions, common denominators are used broadly to mean getting to a shared characteristic that allows a valid comparison between seemingly unlike things.

So it turns out that apples and oranges *can* be compared to each other if the common denominator is fruit sales. In this almost-too-easy example, the common denominator becomes fruit because it allows comparison of the two. The common denominator can also be trees or juice, which are other ways that apples and oranges share a category. You're likely thinking that that is a funny example but not realistic. Try this: you're going to invest in a fruit orchard and want to compare the relative impact of climate change on orange tree yield and apple tree yield before you decide which one to invest in.

There are situations that require all manner of data comparisons. However, the further you have to reach to find a common denominator (both apples and oranges are fruit but are also plants; both are also living things; both also live on Earth), the less likely your comparisons will be relevant.

Weighting

You may have heard terms like "weighted scores" or "weighted average." Weighting is the process of increasing the contribution of some data points over others (it comes from the idea of adding some weight to one side of a balanced scale). In practice, continuing the apples and oranges example, you might know that you can sell an orange for 1.2 times what you can sell an apple for. That may cause you to assign a higher weight to the value of your orange count than that of your apple count. In practice, weighting is most often used in survey or marketing analysis by helping make the sample more like the population, but it can inform the conclusions of any data set as needed.

Anecdote: TQM

I learned about total quality management (TQM) back in the early 1980s (also called quality circles). American companies had turned to Japanese companies for the methods and processes that could improve the quality of goods and services. Those techniques led to the more recent Six Sigma program for using data to understand defects.

7

HOW TO IMPROVE

If you're any good at all, you know you can be better.

— LINDSAY BUCKINGHAM

A chieving goals within a process usually means improving the performance of that process. Specifically it means some change in the thing, the specification, or the time, which will result in performance improvement. The path to performance improvement starts with knowing where you are now and deciding where you want to go.

Where You Are Now

Assess your current state through a combination of the baseline of your process success data (KPI data), your process capability, and anything you know of that might be changing in the environment. The current state for Success Coffee could be that through our strategies, we're meeting our revenue and cost goals, our processes are stable, and there are no new coffee shops coming into our neighborhood. The current state for your organization is similarly defined by the KPIs at every level of your KPI map. Your revenue numbers, margin performance, and the successful outcomes of your processes tell the story of your current state. And whenever you need to know more about something, your KPI map provides a way to drill down into the sources of each of those measures to identify the major contributors to the current state.

How You Got There

Root cause analysis is a combination of brainstorming and data analysis regarding a pattern of performance (usually defects). As I mentioned, a report of data and the interpretation of that data are separate activities. So the defect data isn't useful until you determine what that defect data *means*, and we get there through root cause analysis. In practice, root cause analysis is structured brainstorming about the source of a problem followed by validation of your conclusions in the data. Alternately, root cause analysis can be finding an unexpected pattern in your data, then working backward to tell the story about why that's happening. In either case, it's a partnership between quantitative analysis (data) and qualitative analysis (brainstorming).

One of my favorite root cause analysis methods is the **five whys** method. When you have the answer to that first "why," you ask the second one about why *that* condition exists, and so on until you've asked (and answered) five times. The rule of thumb is that if you continue asking why, you'll get to the real root cause. Whether it takes fewer than five or more than five, the value of this method is that the more you ask, the more information you're going to uncover.

I have a cup of coffee every morning and rarely enjoy it (defect = lack of enjoyment).

1. **Why** aren't I enjoying my coffee? Because the coffee has gone cold.
2. **Why** has the coffee gone cold? Because it's been sitting in the cup for the past hour.
3. **Why** has it been sitting in the cup for the past hour? Because I had to shower and get ready for work.
4. **Why** did the coffee sit untouched while I got ready for work? Because I poured it as soon as I got up.
5. **Why** didn't I pour it when I got out of the shower? Because I tell myself that I need a cup of coffee to wake up enough to get into the shower and get dressed. Clearly that's not true since I'm not drinking it.

Root cause of non-enjoyable coffee: pouring the coffee long before I'm going to drink it. Here, the five whys is pointing me to a simple restructuring of my morning routine.

Often called a fishbone, a **cause and effect diagram** is so named because it looks vaguely like the skeleton of a fish once it's drawn. Traditionally, the "head" of the fish (where you write the problem you're trying to solve) goes on the left, and a straight line (the "spine" of the fish) is drawn across the rest of the page. Branching lines are drawn from the spine and used to categorize the brainstorm effort. Common categories are people, processes, and tools, although more categories may reveal themselves in the brainstorm. The action is to lead a brainstorm session (or brainstorm on your own) that is similar to the process of asking the five whys. This tool is great for exploring cause and effect where the effect is the problem you're trying to solve.

Pareto analysis and Pareto charts, which I described already, also represent a kind of root cause analysis. You'll recall that I mentioned Vilfredo Pareto (*such* a fun name to say out loud), who did research on landowners in Italy in the early twentieth century. The rule of thumb that 80 percent of effects come from 20 percent of causes is attributed to Pareto's research and is surprisingly true much of the time (although I'm sure there is some mathematical reason why it's true so often). What that means for you and me is that by understanding what categories or sources make up 80 percent of our defects, we're likely to find a relatively small (20 percent of causes) root cause.

Pareto analysis goes something like this:

- We have a goal to reduce safety incidents by 10 percent (from 200 to 180) by the end of the year.
- There are five different kinds of incidents: slips and falls, muscle strains, repetitive stress, hit by a falling object, and inhaling toxic fumes.
- Inhaling toxic fumes makes up 80 percent of all safety incidents (160 incidents last year).
- To reduce the overall incident count by 10 percent (twenty incidents), we will have to reduce inhaling toxic fumes by 12.5 percent (from 160 to 140).

So this goal statement, in contrast to "reduce safety incidents by 10 percent," is much more precise with the target of "reducing overall safety incidents by 10 percent by reducing inhaling toxic fumes by 20 percent." We've also ensured that by putting our improvement efforts toward the greatest defect contributor, we have the best chance of overall improvement.

Definition: Low-Hanging Fruit

This term can have the negative connotation of being the easy way out. But in process improvement, the lowest-hanging fruit has the greatest return on the time or resource investment, which is a good thing.

Pareto analysis is often called "low-hanging fruit" to describe an improvement that is easiest to get to (also often known as "quick wins" or the most-bang-for-your-buck approach to improvement). I think of this also as the wonderfully lazy approach to improvement. What is the greatest measurable improvement I can get for the least amount of effort? The reason for seeking the easiest improvement first can be that the benefit greatly outweighs the cost. If we get super nerdy about the low-hanging fruit, we could say that our basic need is to provide fuel to our bodies. The lowest-hanging fruit has no need for a ladder and a lower commitment of calorie burn to get fuel. So getting that fruit first allows us to build a calorie buffer to pursue more difficult fruits. Similarly in organizations, getting the quick wins out of the way can build up a buffer in the process that makes more difficult improvement objectives easier.

Where You Want to Go

Where you want to go is, by definition, the goals you've set. Sometimes these are set using statistical or process capability methods. Sometimes goals are also set by a seemingly random percentage applied to the current state, leaving you with the expectation of defining the path from the current state to that imposed goal. Regardless of how the goals are set, your tactics will change based on the amount of change necessary to get there.

Tip!
If you want significant changes in your results, make significant changes in your process.

Small-Scale vs. Large-Scale Change

While it's a great idea to set goals within the statistical guardrails of past process performance, getting goal setters to understand and work within those limits is an uphill battle in an organization where statistical rigor is uncommon. However, know that if you set targets *outside* of the statistical limits, you're much more likely to be successful if you make comprehensive changes to the process to achieve them. The point here is that if you want to get significant changes in your results, you'll have to make significant changes in your process.

Making improvements within the limits of what's

happened before is typically incremental, while those that come with transformational process change are comprehensive. This is to say you can seek small progressive performance changes over time or a large-scale performance change through process change. Since everything we do is a process, improvement means process improvement. Recalling that our success measure is "thing + specification + time," our three areas to improve are the thing, the spec, or the time.

Incremental improvement—also called continuous improvement—is a proven method of getting good results over time by making constant small changes in the specification or the time it takes. The good news is that a myriad of variables will continue to drive variation in your processes. Everything from seasonal temperature change (which will have an impact on things you'd never expect), to aging equipment, to fluctuations in your workforce, will all bring about variations in your processes. Incremental improvement keeps you focused on always doing better without having to make huge changes.

Comprehensive improvement—If incremental improvement is small adjustments to drive sustainable improvement *within* statistical limits, comprehensive improvement is large improvements in an overall process to change the mean performance and therefore the limits themselves. It's common to want to use incremental methods to accomplish comprehensive process change, which is a great way to ensure that you'll spend valuable analysis effort explaining why you failed to meet your goals rather than analyzing improvement opportunities. Here's the bottom line for improvement: if you want big results, you'll have to make big changes.

The calculations of statistical limits are (of course) entirely relative: the range of acceptable variance in ball bearing manufacturing is much smaller than the range of acceptable variance for walking to the coffee shop. It's important only when you know that you're asking more from your process than it's ever produced before and are making plans for how you'll support that.

How You Can Get There

As always, this comes back to processes. Think back to the shopping list you made in chapter 3. It was an inefficient shopping list because you made the list from memory and searched the store for each item as it appeared on the list. This had you getting an onion from the produce section, then getting some cheese from the dairy section, then heading back to produce for some celery. What if you wanted to improve the performance of that process? Let's assume that your objective is to get all the items on your list as quickly as possible. That objective cries out for removing wasted time.

The low-hanging fruit here is to take your original list and group the items based on where they are in the grocery store. So your produce will be together, cheese (there's always cheese) and other dairy products will be together, meat (if that's your thing) will also be together. OK, now you've got an ordered list—in this case ordered by location within the store. You could have as easily ordered the list by how expensive items were or by how critical they were. In the success formula (thing + specification + time = success), we've held thing (buy everything on the list) and the specification (specified amount of money or less) stable while improving the time it takes to complete the process. Process improvement—check.

Taking Aim

Meeting a goal means taking some specific action. I imagine you (like I) have been part of improvement initiatives that amounted to "do better" (which includes "do more," "do faster," and other classics). Here's the thing you know but may not have said out loud: those initiatives fail because they're not initiatives; they're admonitions or warnings. What you want to improve is a process, and because a process is a thing that happens in steps and in time, you have to take *specific* action to change something.

Improving performance, once you've isolated the enabling indicators and subprocesses, is a matter of understanding the root cause (or *a* root cause—there are often more than one) and taking specific corrective action. In a perfect world, this corrective action then becomes part of the official process, and improvements are sustained. Identifying the right tactic means finding the primary enabling indicator, determining why it's not performing where you want, then updating it.

Strengthening Good instead of Fixing Bad

The core of most business measurement is identifying defects and fixing them. In fact, some of the best innovation comes from reclassifying something from an acceptable defect to an unacceptable one. There are lots of great examples of businesses getting closer and closer to mathematical perfection by driving defects out of their processes. In fact, Japanese automakers introduced the idea of zero-defect process improvement to continuously chip away at imperfection. This is exactly as awesome as it sounds.

Definition: Zero Defects

Zero defects is a combination goal model and motivation method. Whether possible in real life or not, organizations with a zero-defect approach don't accept any level (or any type) of defect as inevitable.

There is also another way.

When the performance you're working to improve includes human behavior, it's much easier to get improvement by reinforcing strengths than by eliminating defects. Not to say that defects don't need to be fixed—they do. But focusing on only defects can limit growth. Most companies, through performance goals, have established what the minimum performance expectation is for their employees.

Through job descriptions, competency models, and training, they ensure that employees can perform at that minimum performance expectation. As a result, most performance management—in practice, if not in design—consists of identifying root causes for and correcting those defects.

Once we know those performance misses (defects), we can apply some corrective action that will bring that performance up to the minimum expectation. Because processes are ongoing, there is always a new batch of defects to be managed, and this seems like success for a while. But at some point, you realize that what you've done is corrected all the defects to be sure they meet the minimum bar. If you're exceptionally good at this, you will have institutionalized minimum performance. I call this "managing to mediocrity." The trick is to identify data points both below *and* above that minimum line.

~

Definition: Classical Conditioning

Classical conditioning is the psychological concept that includes positive reinforcement, negative reinforcement, and punishment. Studies have consistently shown that changes in behavior are faster and longer lasting when you reinforce positive behavior rather than work to extinguish negative behavior.

With this information, you split your effort evenly into correcting defects (you'll miss some) and strengthening successes (you'll miss some of these too). Bolstering a strength is an easier path than extinguishing a defect in behavior, so your net return on that effort will be higher by making sure you're working on both.

How to Improve at Success Coffee

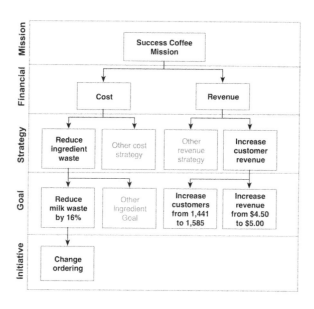

We know a lot about Success Coffee at this point. We've established a mission, strategies to realize that mission, and goals to improve.

Success Coffee Mission

We build community by offering fresh-baked muffins and fresh-roasted espresso drinks in our neighborhood.

Financial KPIs:

1. Gross margin: total revenue minus total cost
2. Revenue: money received for all beverages and muffins sold
3. Cost (direct): money spent on preparing and selling beverages and muffins.

KPI Strategies:

1. Increase average revenue per customer
2. Increase number of customers
3. Reduce ingredient waste

Enabling Indicators (for this set of strategies):

1. Average number of customers per week (we treat customers and transactions as the same number, though we know there are flaws in either choice)
2. Revenue per customer
3. Milk waste (gallons of expired—and therefore unused—milk; we're not counting milk wasted in the process of making a drink)

Goals:

1. 10 percent increase in the number of customers
2. $0.50 increase in revenue per customer
3. Reduce milk waste by 16 percent

Strategy 1: Increase Number of Customers

Process to improve: Customer acquisition at Success Coffee comes from our marketing process. We have quarterly ads in the local paper but don't do any other advertising.

Enabling indicator: Average number of customers per week.

Baseline: For the past twelve months, we've averaged 1,441 customers per month across the seven days that we're open. We track this through our point-of-sale system that tracks transactions. Rather than try to parse whether someone picking up coffee for herself and four other people counts as one customer or five customers, we rely on "transaction" to define "customer." Our baseline is an average of 1,441 customers per week with a calculated upper limit of 1,913 and lower control limit of 1,025.

Goal: Increase average customers per month by 10 percent by reaching out to clubs. A 10 percent increase in our current average of 1,441 is well within our control limits. So our existing processes should be able to meet an average monthly target from 1,441 to 1,585 through incremental improvement in the thing, the specification, or the time rather than requiring some process transformation.

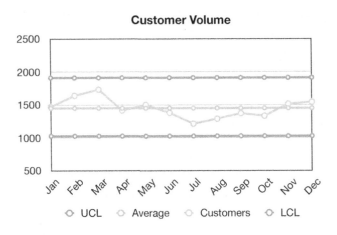

Customer Volume

Tactic: Target advertising to local book clubs for meeting space. Our current advertising process is targeted to a wide audience. So we'll add to that by also advertising specifically to local book clubs to offer them meeting space on our lower-volume days.

Strategy 2: Increase Average Customer Revenue

Process to improve: We have a passive sales process including signage and counter display. Our employees also make specific recommendations for a more active sales process, but that's not in scope for this improvement.

Enabling indicator: Average revenue per customer (transaction) per visit. Each transaction in our point-of-sale system has a transaction number, allowing easy calculation of the average. We know also that the flaw (because all measures are flawed in some way) is that when there are two people in line but only one of them pays, the definition of customer becomes "paying customer" instead of "coffee-drinking customer."

Tip!
Beware of averages, and be extra wary of averages of averages. They hide all manner of important details.

Baseline: For the past twelve months, the average revenue per customer has been $4.53. There are 1,441 customers in a month and all buy a beverage. The average beverage cost of $3.50 multiplied by 1,441 customers delivers an average monthly revenue of $5,043.50. Half of those folks (721) also buy a muffin, which costs $2.00. So our average muffin revenue for the month is $1,441. Total average monthly revenue (coffee +

muffins) is $7,926, and that divided by our 1,441 customers gets us to that baseline.

I want to note here that I've got averages and averages of averages. While this makes the math easy, a lot of variability can hide in those averages that can be either a missed opportunity or can prevent me from meeting my goal. It's also possible due to rounding that the pennies may be off.

We're also assuming in this data that the numbers are evenly spread across all days and weeks of the month. If 40 percent of those customers come in on Mondays, and our analysis misses that, we may fail to increase staff on Mondays to accommodate the increase in customers. We may also decide to have a strategy to even out the volume per day rather than just increase across the entire week.

Goal: Increase the average revenue per customer from $4.50 to $5.00 by selling muffins to more than 50 percent of customers. While our process includes the staff making recommendations, we don't want to slow down our process by asking our staff to focus heavily on making recommendations. There is plenty of research in the power of suggestion ("Would you like to supersize that?"), but we're sensitive to overt sales tactics with our customers and will focus first on passive sales.

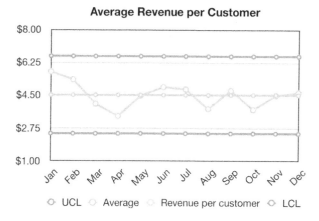

Average Revenue per Customer

◌ UCL   ◌ Average   Revenue per customer   ◌ LCL

Tactic: Increase the 50 percent of customers who buy a muffin to 75 percent through increased passive advertising. What we know is that the blueberry muffins sell out every day, and the banana nut muffins rarely do. So rather than just posting the label and price of our muffins, we'll create new signage that we bake all our muffins fresh each morning, and we will increase our production of blueberry muffins.

Strategy 3: Reduce Direct Costs

Process to improve: Making coffee drinks that have milk. Steaming milk in a pitcher requires more milk than necessary in the pitcher, so a few ounces are always wasted. Milk is also wasted when an unopened carton goes past its expiration date before it can be used, so it's poured down the drain.

Enabling indicator: Milk that's thrown away because it has expired. Most commonly at Success Coffee, this is milk that is never opened and then thrown away because it expires. Less common but still a problem is milk that we open and begin using for some drinks, but then it expires before it is all used.

Baseline: For the past twelve months, an average of thirty-one (half-gallon) cartons of milk expire and are poured out each month. In that twelve months, we had a really bad month in June, when we threw away seventy-three cartons of expired milk. That outlier skewed our data so heavily that I took it out for calculating the process capability.

The statisticians quibble about whether to remove outliers, and rather than explain (or engage in) those arguments, this is a place to trust our knowledge as much as the data. If the outlier—in this case, seventy-three cartons of expired milk—isn't clearly understood or is likely to happen again, leave it in because it represents your real situation and means that your goal might be just to get more predictable performance by reducing that variation.

If the outlier is an exception with a clear cause, it may be fine to omit it. In this case, our main refrigerator failed, and the milk all went bad overnight. We replaced that refrigerator, so we have some years before something like that can happen again. The key point here is to remember that it's OK to bring a little common sense into the equation. So we take the outlier out and calculate our process capability without it.

Goal: Our goal is to reduce milk waste (for expired milk) by 16 percent from an average of thirty-one half-gallon cartons per month to about twenty-six half-gallon cartons per month. This goal is below the process capability (the lower control limit—the average minus three standard deviation—is nine), so we're committing not just to an aggressive target but to making transformational change to the process itself.

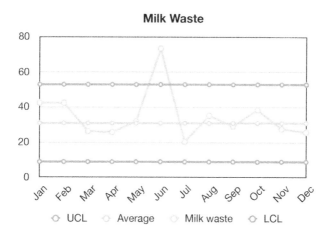

Tactic: We'll change our order frequency to two times weekly rather than one time weekly and will estimate low when we aren't sure. When at risk of running out, one of our staff will go to the local store for more milk. This tactic has some risks associated with it, which is the nature of transformational change, so we'll track all the details and keep in close contact with the staff to see what works.

There you have it. The ultimate answer to the question "How will we realize our mission?" is as follows: by increasing customers, increasing customer revenue, and reducing milk waste. We arrived at these choices by finding the improvements most likely to improve our KPIs. Like any set of tactics, these will need to be monitored to be sure there are no hidden problems. We can be assured that these strategies, goals, and tactics are clearly aimed at our solutions.

8

NOW WHAT?

The way to get started is to quit talking and begin doing.

— WALT DISNEY

B ack in the beginning of this book, I told you how the VP of sales in a previous role asked me what my ideas were for meeting the increased sales quotas. I developed a plan using the sales conversion rate (the percentage of leads that become sales), the sales cycle time (how long it takes to close a sale), and the average revenue per sale. With some basic math, I told him how many dollars in deals needed to be in the sales pipeline each month to achieve those goals.

He didn't bite because he trusted his instincts more than the sales data. He had plans to pursue a completely different kind of business, so he didn't want to be held back by past data.

The problem wasn't with my data—it was clear and

historically accurate. The problem wasn't that I was super-smart and he wasn't. The problem was that I didn't meet that leader at his vision. His vision was for transformational change in the process; he saw revenue from new kinds of customers and needed a new process for getting there. What I proposed was working within the current process to get a better outcome. And let's be clear: I was right. If he wanted to know how to get the most out of the current situation, I was right. Remember that success is relative. The problem was that I didn't take time to work with that leader to understand *his* definition of success.

So I missed an opportunity to use data and process knowledge to work with that leader to build a path to his vision. Given the opportunity again, I would start with his mission and work backward into the financial metrics, the strategies, and the goals before I started working on tactics. That's why this book starts at mission and not at KPIs.

You can have all the data, all the process, all the goals and tactics, and be entirely *right* while still missing a chance for meaningful change in your organization. Everything in this book gives you tools to set up (or discover) KPIs for pretty much any organization. A peanut butter and jelly sandwich process can stand in for a manufacturing process, customer service transaction process, or software development. Find your mission, then build a bridge to making it true.